An Almighty Passion

Alan Hargrave was born in a terraced house in the middle of Leeds – an area now buried under university and inner-city motorway. He trained as a Chemical Engineer before working for ten years with the Anglican Church in South America – first on a development project with indigenous people in northern Argentina, then planting churches in Bolivia. He returned to the UK in 1987 to train for ordained ministry. In 1994 he became the first Vicar of Holy Cross, a new parish on a council estate on the edge of Cambridge. He is passionate about mission, unity, justice, cricket, golf, narrowboats, his four children and Annie.

An Almighty Passion

Meeting God in Ordinary Life

Alan Hargrave

to Mary with love & prayers

God bless

Alan

Published in Great Britain in 2002 by
Triangle
SPCK
Holy Trinity Church
Marylebone Road
London NW1 4DU

British Library Cataloguing-in-Publication Data

A catalogue record for this book is available from the British Library

ISBN 0-281-05451-7

Typeset by Kenneth Burnley, Wirral, Cheshire
Printed in Great Britain by
Omnia Books, Glasgow

Contents

In memory of my dad,
who told us stories of Great Grandma Stead
and Jeffrey Lister,
which still live on inside us.

Thank You

Thou that hast giv'n so much to me
Give one thing more, a grateful heart.
George Herbert

Far too many people have contributed to this book to thank them all. I am particularly grateful to the people of Holy Cross and East Barnwell for letting me have four months off to write it, as well as to Philipa and Jonathan who stepped into the breach. Thank you to Susan, John, Deb, David, Sylvia and Henry – honest and encouraging readers of the draft. I would specially like to thank Alan Boyd, visionary, anorak and great mate; Ann Morisy, prophet; and Annie, who held the objective view and did not call me a hero when I swatted a mosquito.

Most of all, I am deeply grateful to all those ordinary people who have inspired me to write this book. Many of them think they are rubbish, but actually they are the ones in whom I met the living God.

Introduction

As I grow older I believe more and more in less and less. Less and less in the secondary issues of faith (which are often divisive). More and more in the great doctrines of Trinity, Incarnation, Passion and Resurrection (which have been at the heart of Christian understanding of God since the early centuries of the Church).

Unfortunately doctrine is not very sexy these days. It smacks of being dogmatic, closed, bigoted even. Yet these doctrines are for me the vital substance of life. They make sense of my life experience and of my ministry. They feed my great passions: our mission to share God's astonishing love and amazing grace in Christ; a deep desire for unity and community; a thirst for justice and a concern for the vulnerable and the forgotten; the enabling and equipping of ministers, lay and ordained, female and male, from all walks of life, to further Christ's mission.

These are passions to which I am deeply committed. They are rooted in biblical reflection, following a wide experience of life and ministry, particularly in Argentina, Bolivia and on a housing estate which would not fit most people's image of Cambridge. This has brought me face to face with people of different cultures, traditions and situations that have greatly enriched, challenged and deepened my faith. It has forced me to read the Bible again through new eyes. I went to these communities to share with them my faith in the God who has revealed himself in Christ. However, it was there, in the most unlikely of people and situations, that Christ revealed himself to me.

Introduction

This book is about the great doctrines of God. It is not an exposition of those doctrines. It does not seek to defend or expound them. It simply seeks to relate them to the pain and the joy, the mundane and the surprising, the dull and the dramatic of the everyday life in which God Incarnate is to be found.

Before You Start

No todas las cosas que suceden son buenas para contar: acciones hay que por grandes deben callarse, y otras que por bajas no deben decirse.

(Not everything that happens is good to relate. There are some things so noble that it's better not to speak of them, and others, so low that it's better not to speak of them either.)

Cervantes

A couple arrive one evening at a vicarage door. They have been trying for a baby for a long time and, last week, after a difficult pregnancy and all the fears that go along with it, a perfect baby girl is born. As they stand at the doorstep, gazing down in wonder at the small bundle in their arms, the door opens. 'Oh hello,' says the vicar, 'can I help you?'

They look awkwardly at one another as if they don't quite know what to say. 'Have you come to see about baptism?' asks the vicar, helpfully. 'Well,' replies the young man, haltingly, holding up the bundle for the vicar to see, 'we're not really sure. The thing is, we just want to say thank you to somebody.'

The experience of that couple mirrors what happens to most of us from time to time. Powerful experiences lead us beyond ourselves, but we are not sure what to do with them, where to put them. As T. S. Eliot says: 'We had the experience but missed the meaning' (from 'The Dry Salvages').

This is a book of stories. They are all true (though names have been changed and situations altered so as to protect confidentiality). It seeks to find meaning in some of the stories which have affected my life; to make connections, without imagining for a moment that they can be exactly located in a category or that all the loose ends can be tied up. These are not stories about saints, heroes or 'Little Miss Perfect', but about very ordinary people struggling with all the pressures ordinary life brings. It is through such encounters that God has met me in Trinity, Incarnation, Passion and Resurrection.

Some of the most profound experiences are not included here, since they are, by their very nature, too painful or too difficult to disguise.

I have deliberately left explanation to a minimum. Just as with Jesus' parables, and indeed with his life, the theology is in the story itself. The danger is that over-dissection can strip out the power and the mystery.

Working with 'trainee vicars' in the parish has been somewhat salutary. Capable students, who write quality essays in front of computer screens, surrounded by books, are often at a loss when it comes to making theological sense of real life. That difficult funeral, the disturbing thing the 8-year-old said in the school assembly, the man who leads our prayers so powerfully and honestly but who is a hopeless alcoholic, the planned closure of the local secondary school, that amazing concert at the Leper Chapel in response to homelessness – are these just unconnected events or do they 'fit' somewhere?

My primary aim is to try and locate experience within a clear theological framework through biblical reflection. The point is not just to allow text to interact with text, but to allow text to interact with life.

The few encounters related here by no means exhaust the depths of the great doctrines which lead us into the heart of God. More than anything, I hope that, as you read these stories, ponder the quotations and make your own connections, they will trigger, in your mind and heart, your own stories, through which you yourself, perhaps without realizing it, have met the living God in Trinity, Incarnation, Passion and Resurrection.

> *Theology has the mission of seeking out answers to new and urgent problems. The deposit of faith is not a stagnant cistern. It is a Spring of Living Water.*
>
> Boff, 1986

Acknowledgements

The publishers acknowledge with thanks permission to reproduce extracts from the following:

T. S. Eliot, 'The Dry Salvages', from *The Four Quartets*, published by Faber and Faber Ltd.

'Fire and Ice', from *The Poetry of Robert Frost*, edited by Edward Connery Lathem, the Estate of Robert Frost and Jonathan Cape as publisher. Used by permission of The Random House Group Limited.

Philip Larkin, 'An Arundel Tomb', from *Collected Poems*, published by Faber and Faber Ltd.

I

Trinity

I bind unto myself today
The strong name of the Trinity
By invocation of the same
The three in one
And one in three.

From 'St Patrick's Breastplate'

A word of introduction . . .

There was a time when theologians showed little interest in the doctrine of the Trinity. In recent years all this has changed.

Cocksworth, 1997

For centuries the doctrine of the Trinity has been the touchstone of Orthodoxy for the Christian Church. Classically it affirms that there is only one God, but that God exists in three 'persons' – Father, Son and Holy Spirit. Although there are no neat biblical texts that clearly define the doctrine, we cannot help but conclude, as we read the scriptures, that Father, Son and Spirit are all God, and that God is one.

Unfortunately, long battles to root out every kind of heresy meant that the doctrine became the preserve of the theological and ecclesiastical élite – the sort of thing that people dabbled in at their peril. One religious order, for a time in its history, insisted that on Trinity Sunday no sermon was to be preached, due to the difficulty of the subject matter.

But the doctrine of the Trinity is far too important for us to ignore. And indeed, it has been making a comeback! In recent times theologians have rediscovered the importance of the Trinity, particularly with regard to relationships. And aren't relationships at the heart of everything? We can get to the moon, put millions of 'bits' of information on a microscopic chip, transplant a heart. But we can't stand the neighbours, live in peace with people from a different ethnic background, share out fairly the abundance God has given us or even get on with our husband or wife, the one person we have chosen above all others to live with.

Relationships are at the very heart of the Trinity. For God does not exist as an isolated individual, who made us only to avoid being lonely. On the contrary. In the beginning – before all time, from everlasting to everlasting, in love and unity, in trust and harmony, in tenderness and delight, in loudness and laughter, in pain and in anguish – is God, not alone, but in relationship. A relationship of indescribable intimacy and passion, so close that we rightly affirm that God is one. Yet it is a relationship not of one alone, but of the three: Father, Son and Holy Spirit, melting, blending, penetrating, flowing together to produce a united creative capacity far greater than the sum of the parts, yet where individual integrity is never entirely lost. (See Isaac Asimov's description of the Triads in his science fiction novel *The Gods Themselves*.)

And God makes humankind in his own image. Not man alone, but male and female together. *We* are intimately linked to the relationships within the Trinity. Many theologians these days believe that we should think of the Holy Spirit as female. I am not sure if God has sex, but the intimacy of the Trinity is probably something between the passionate embrace of lovers and the warm tenderness of parents with a new-born child. Not quite 'Mum, dad and the kid(s)', but perhaps more like that than the static, dispassionate, detached, distant picture of God-in-Heaven we tend to see portrayed.

This unity is not, as someone once described the nuclear family, 'selfishness for three'. It is an outgoing love, a love which, knowing the risk, cannot but create and cannot but include the creation in the joy, wonder, mystery and communion God has known from all eternity. It is a love which delights in beauty and abundance. A love which never gives up on its children, no matter how far from that love they have strayed. It is a love which is the source of all creativity, of all unity, of all community, of all generosity, of all that is best on the earth and in the heavens.

We are made in this image, and though it has become marred in us, it has never been lost. It is still clearly visible in creation. All that is best in humanity springs from this creator God who, from all eternity, is Father, Son and Holy Spirit, the three in one, and one in three. And belief in such a God is not a matter of intellectual assent but, as Karl Barth (the great Swiss theologian who was at the forefront of the Church's opposition to Hitler) says, it is an 'encounter' (Barth, 1949, p. 15) resulting in risky, committed action, which is what faith is all about.

Unity

I pray that all those who believe may be completely united, just as you and I are completely united, Father, I in them and you in me, perfectly one, so that the whole world will know that you sent me and that you love them just as much as you love me.

Jesus' prayer on the night before he was crucified, from John 17

East Barnwell is not most people's idea of Cambridge. Forget the dreaming spires. This is a very ordinary council estate, built mostly since the war. The churches here are far removed from the fan-vaulted perpendicular glory of King's College chapel. They are multi-purpose, utilitarian, brick (or in one case tin) boxes with useful space but nothing aesthetically pleasing to commend them. Four small churches serving a community of around 7,000 people.

In recent years we have steadily drawn closer together. There are painful memories of hurt and rejection from the past that make this difficult. Yet over time we have grown to respect each other and begun to believe that we can indeed receive and learn from one another. Not only that but we have begun to see that we can accomplish so much more together than we can individually. It began with a joint service on Christmas Day, initially between the Baptists and the Methodists. Then a united meditation and march between all the churches on Good Friday. Joint evening worship every month and united study groups followed. In 1999 we signed a 'Covenant' – an agreement to worship and to work together as we reach out in Christ's name for the benefit of our community. Then we held a united mission to East Barnwell and a weekend away together to seek God's way forward for the future.

The weekend away proves a great success. A number of people have declined to come because of difficulties travelling or uncertainties about the accommodation. However, an elderly woman from one of the churches bucks the trend. She cannot sit down without being in pain, and standing is even worse. She walks with a zimmer at a speed which makes the action replay look fast. As a result she is late for every session. And yet her very presence and determination inspire us. 'If Alice can do it we can all do it' I hear people say in the corridors. I look down the hall to see if anyone else is coming before we begin lunch. There she is. Still 30 yards and several minutes to go. She is being led along by a 4-year-old called Jack with whom she has struck up a rapport. Yes, if Alice can do it, we *can* do it, I say to myself.

Ecumenism, in our case, is not a 'top-down' exercise. Members of the different churches are involved together in community outreach to children, young people, parents, the elderly. They meet each other at the post office, at school and on the No. 3 bus.

But the big question remains. Should we remain as 'just good friends' or should we become a single, united church? At Holy Cross the church council considers the issue and decides to put it to the whole church. Instead of a sermon we hold a discussion. What has been our experience of working together? What are our hopes and fears for the future?

There are plenty of positive comments. Then George starts. 'Why can't we just be C of E, like we always have been?' 'What will happen to our building?' 'Why do we need to change?' 'Aren't we better off as we are?' 'Won't we lose our identity in some happy-clappy free for all?'

I try and answer patiently as best I can but mostly I just listen and acknowledge the concerns. I tell myself that these things are better spoken than left unsaid and that they probably represent the views of a number who would never stand up and say them in public, only in the car park afterwards. But inside my heart sinks.

Finally the discussion draws to a close. I hope that it will at least be clear – not a 45 per cent/55 per cent split that will only divide us. We say a prayer, leave a bit of silence and then it is time to vote. The question is: 'Do you believe that God is calling us to become a single united church with the other East Barnwell churches?'

Those in favour?

I look around in disbelief. To my utter astonishment every single hand is raised. George's hand is one of the first to go up! No one is against. There are no abstentions. It is completely unanimous.

It is a family service. The children are in (and voting). As always, there has been a fair bit of 'background noise'. But now there is complete silence. Several people are weeping quietly. I am completely at a loss as to what to say or do next.

We are a very diverse group indeed – different ages, stages, situations. But for a moment, it as though we have experienced something of the unity, the harmony, the love and the trust of Father, Son and Holy Spirit, tangibly in our midst.

I pray to God that unity may happen soon. There are still many obstacles in the way. I know that the road will not be easy. We will, no doubt, fall out again before too long.

But for now, for an instant, we have glimpsed the Trinity.

Extravagant Creation

The wolf shall live with the lamb
Leopards will lie down with young goats
Calves and lion cubs will feed together
And a small child shall lead them.

Isaiah 11.6

I began to dance. Slowly, slowly at first and then going with the music, faster I danced, and faster until I went beyond. I danced every dance I knew and dances unknown to me. I danced and danced until the music had to keep up with me. I was the master of this music. I felt myself alive and unfearful. Every part of me, every limb, every muscle energised in this dance. For how long I danced or how long I laughed I cannot tell. But it seemed that I would be dancing for ever.

Keenan, 1992

We have been looking forward to seeing the Queen Elizabeth Game Park, and it does not disappoint us. The hippos, in particular, are wonderful. But wherever we travel in south-western Uganda, the countryside is lush and green. There are lakes and hills bursting with life. I am bowled over by the astonishing variety of birds of every shape, size, colour and kind. If the Garden of Eden did indeed exist, maybe it was here?

We are full of this sense of abundance as we attend the Sunday morning service in Kambuga. I had a sneaking suspicion and, sure enough, as we arrive at the church door, I am whisked away to the vestry where I am informed that I will be preaching. My friend, Eric, will translate. This time I am not unprepared. I have resurrected an old sermon about the feeding of the 5,000 based on the account in John's Gospel. St John gives us an important detail the other Gospels lack. He tells us that the five loaves and two fishes are, in fact, provided by a small, insignificant boy, whose name we do not know. But his paltry offering is not rejected as worthless by Jesus. Instead, it is transformed to become the means of blessing for a huge crowd of hungry people.

The service is 'Morning Prayer' with what looks like *Hymns Ancient and Modern* translated into 'Ruchiga'. Except that there's no organ, just a 10-year-old girl with a big drum, and a slightly older boy with a slightly smaller one. As we walk into this large, tin church it's disappointing to see the small congregation – only about 40 or so. However, as we start to get going people pour in. After half an hour there are several hundred, with more still arriving.

A hymn is announced. Eric shows me the page in the book. The titles, at least, are in English. It's 'Rock of Ages Cleft for Me'. Ah! I know this one. At least I'll be able to follow the tune and maybe sing some of the words. However, when the music starts, it is like no tune and no version of 'Rock of Ages' I have ever heard. The drums beat and the woman next to the drummer-girl sings the lead. The congregation sing back in reply, clapping and swaying with the music.

Then, from nowhere, a small boy appears. He looks about 5, or 6 at the most. There he is, right at the front, between the choir stalls, quite unselfconscious, dancing. At the end of the 'hymn' he disappears back to his place. There is a reading, a prayer, then another hymn. Back he comes. He is dancing in perfect step with the music. He is part of the music, leading the music. This is no childish attempt at aping adults. This is a boy who knows how to dance, who is master of the dance. This is a dance of authority and power. It is a dance of rhythm and balance. This is a boy who, like David, is dancing before the Lord.

Again and again, every time we sing, he appears at the front of the church and dances. When we get to the collection the service has been in progress for nearly three hours. The time seems to have flown. I think of services I have attended where, after half an hour, I am desperate to leave. I feel sympathy for some of our baptism families. At the end of the service they rush for the car park and light up a fag, inhaling deeply. But this service is not like that at all.

The collection itself lasts well over half an hour. Each small community from the surrounding district gives in turn. The woman with the collection basket goes to the back of the church and people come forward, putting in their money, or bringing their bag of sweet potatoes, a stalk of bananas, avocado pears, sugar cane, a bag of cement or whatever they have to offer. The produce will be auctioned off later in the service, an event in itself. The music starts up and they begin to dance from the distant back of this large church towards the altar. Down the aisle they come, clapping and laughing, carrying the fruit of God's extravagant blessing, bringing untold riches out of poverty. And there to lead them, every single time, is the small boy. I take out my camera to get a shot of him. As soon as he sees it he freezes. He becomes a self-conscious small child. I put it away and he immediately resumes as leader of the dance, leader of our worship. My sermon scarcely needs preaching. He *is* the sermon. Like the small boy who provides five loaves and two fish to feed 5,000, this small-boy-from-nowhere has become the source of blessing for all 500 of us gathered here. I learn, later, that he has severe learning difficulties. He has only just begun to speak odd words. Sing, he cannot. Dance, he can. It is as though he cannot help himself.

I think of my brother, a violin maker of international repute, putting the finishing touches to an exact copy of an Andrea Guarneri cello. Every scratch, every fracture in the varnish must be identical. It will be worth several thousand pounds. But, he tells me, he would do it for nothing. He cannot help himself either. The urge to create, the desire to make these instruments, the striving for perfection, is irresistible.

The small boy advances down the aisle followed by the crowd of thankful givers. As they pile up the produce on the altar, it is a picture of the abundance of creation itself. Majestic in its beauty and variety. Extravagantly and joyfully given, over and above the necessary or the pragmatic. Given by the God who cannot help himself, who delights to create, who delights to pour out abundance upon his children. The small boy (whose name turns out to be Emmanuel!) cannot help but dance in response. After all, how could you not worship a God like that?

Praise the Lord all the Earth;
Fire and hail, snow and frost,
Mountains and hills; fruit trees and forests,
Animals, tame and wild; crawling reptiles and birds of the air,
Rulers and peoples; men and women; adults and children.
Let them all praise the name of the Lord,
For he alone is God, and his glory is over the heavens and the earth.

From Psalm 148

Broken Image

So God created human beings in his own image and made them in his own likeness, not man alone, but man and woman together. God blessed them and said: 'Have children, fill the earth and have authority over it.' And God was delighted with the whole of creation, because it was very good.

But the cunning serpent was about to spoil all that . . .

From Genesis 1, 3

I sit in the front room of the community house on the estate. I've been invited by the health visitor to come and share with a group of mums. There are seven or eight of them, almost all single parents with several kids by different partners.

They talk about the nursery school, double glazing, bus fares, *EastEnders* – all the usual stuff. Finally they get round to talking about what it is they really want out of life – and they are all agreed what that is. What they are really longing for is this: a decent bloke who will treat them right, stick with them through thick and thin and be a good dad to the kids. Someone to share their lives with, long term.

In practice this is far from their experience. Maybe it's because of the difficulties of their own home life and the ongoing cycle of broken relationships. Maybe it's because of the abuse and violence some of them have suffered over many years. Maybe it's because the blokes they meet are in the same boat. Whatever the reason, in practice, they just can't seem to make it.

But deep inside, that is what they long for. It's not just about sex. Sex is easy to find. And it's not just about money (though that would be handy). It is about the deep desire for an intimate, long-term relationship with another person.

What they are experiencing is part of what it means to be created in the image of God. To be created for relationship. To know inside that to be fulfilled involves love for another, partnership, communion, intimacy, tenderness.

Tracy, Sharon, Barbara, Samantha and the others are experiencing something of what it means to be made in the image of the Holy Trinity. It is in them, as in all of us, badly damaged and distorted. But it is still there, deeply ingrained. Made, in the image of God.

> *We thinke that Paradise and Calvarie,*
> *Christ's Crosse and Adam's tree stood in one place.*
> *Looke Lord and find both Adams met in me,*
> *As the first Adam's sweat surrounds my face*
> *May the last Adam's blood my soule embrace.*
>
> From 'I shall be made thy musique' by John Donne

Father

Philip said: 'Lord, show us the Father and we will be satisfied.' Jesus replied: 'Look, I've been with you all this time – do you still not realise who I AM? Whoever has seen me has seen the Father.'

John 14.8, 9

Jesus prayed: 'Thank you, Father, that you have hidden these things from the wise and the smart, and have shown them instead to little children.'

Matthew 11.25

It is a big day for Brendan. He is a trainee vicar, but today he is leading the RE lesson for Year 5 at the local state primary school, where he is on placement, balancing academic study with life's realities. These kids have certainly experienced plenty of life's harsh realities between them in their nine years of life.

Brendan has been observing and helping as a classroom assistant for several weeks, and now, encouraged by his excellent classroom teacher, Mr Wilkins, he's having a go at teaching for the first time. 'Well,' says Mr Wilkins, at the end of a busy day, 'Father's Day's coming up, why not do something on the Lord's Prayer – "Our Father"?'

As Brendan thinks about it, an idea begins to develop in his mind. This has been a big term for Brendan. He and his wife had their first child a couple of months ago and the event has dominated and transformed their lives, as it always seems to do.

He begins by reading the Lord's Prayer to the kids. 'Our Father in Heaven . . .' They are a bit fidgety and distracted. Then he pulls out of his pocket a photo. It is a picture of Brendan himself with his tiny daughter, gently curled up in his arms. Brendan is gazing down in love, wonder and pride. The kids suddenly perk up.

'Now,' says, Brendan, 'what do you think this photo says about the relationship between me, as a dad, and my baby daughter?' Hands shoot up. 'She feels all warm and safe, sir.' 'You're looking after her really carefully, sir.' 'She's got pink socks on.' 'You look really proud, sir.' 'You love her, don't you, sir?' 'She needs you to look after her, doesn't she, sir?' 'Do you change her nappy?' 'Cor! I bet it doesn't half stink!' (Raucous laughter.) 'She's looking at you, sir.' 'You're looking at her as well, aren't you sir?'

After a fair bit of discussion Brendan talks about how he believes that God our Father loves us just as much, if not more, than he loves baby Lucy. 'Now,' he says, 'just suppose that you wanted to write a prayer to God the Father, what would you say?'

Hands shoot up, but this isn't the time for answers. Instead he asks the children if they would get out their books and imagine someone wanting to pray to God the Father. What would they say? OK, write it down – ten minutes.

Darren says it's stupid and he doesn't believe in God and he's not doing it. In any case, he hasn't got a father. A girl on the next desk, who seems to be getting on famously, pipes up that she's got four dads! Brendan sympathizes with Darren and agrees that it's fine not to believe in God, but today we are trying to image what someone who *did* believe in God *might* say in a prayer to the Father. Everybody else is scribbling away by now and Darren finally gets down to the business. At the end of ten minutes Brendan calls the class to order. Most have finished, though some are well into page two of massive shopping lists.

'Now you don't have to,' says Brendan, 'but would anyone

like to share with the class what they have written?' Everyone looks around. A few hands go up.

Martin is first up. 'Our Father, please send me a new BMX bike and I hope we win against Milton Road school this afternoon. Amen.' Everybody laughs. He sits down with a grin.

Shelly is next. 'Our Father, we pray for our Mayor and for all the other Mayors, and our MP, and all the other MPs, and the Prime Minister, that they'll all have a lot of luck. Amen.'

Then it's Lisa. 'Dear Father, I thank you for my Mum and Dad and my brothers and sisters and I pray for my Grandma who is having an operation in Addenbrookes. Amen.'

Joel prays: 'Our Father, I am really worried about my sister who didn't come home last night. Please look after her.' He is close to tears as he sits down and some of the kids on his table put their arms around him. The atmosphere has visibly changed. This is serious stuff.

Several more children get up and bring their concerns to the Father. Everyone is joining in the 'Amen.' These no longer sound like the theoretical prayers of someone else. These are the personal and real concerns of 9-year-old kids, brought in earnest to God the Father.

Laura gets up. Her lip is already trembling. Her hands are shaking. 'Are you OK?' asks Mr Wilkins, the teacher, gently. She nods. She wants to read her prayer. 'Dear Father,' she starts, 'please help us.' Hot tears begin to roll down her cheeks. There is complete silence. 'Please help us to find a place to live. It's horrible in the refuge and we need our own home. And please stop Dad from hitting my Mum. Amen.' She sits down, puts her head on her arms, and sobs. All the children on her table put their arms round her. Some of them are crying too.

Heavenly Father, thank you that you love us with all your heart. Hear the prayers of all your children, for their needs are very great. Amen.

Spirit

John said: 'There is someone coming after me who is much more powerful than I am. I am not fit even to undo his sandals. I baptize you with water, but he will baptize you with the Holy Spirit and with fire.'

Luke 3.16, 17

It is the first New Year's Eve in Carboncito. People have moved here from two villages where the land on which they have lived for centuries has been bought up by big companies who are now bulldozing the whole area to plant soya beans. We are meeting in the church for a thanksgiving service. The community has been settled in for several months now. The school and clinic are open. People have work. There is clean water near at hand. Decent houses are being built. The first crops are being harvested. There is a lot to be thankful for.

Unfortunately it is a sweltering night. It has been in the mid-forties (centigrade!) all day and doesn't seem to have cooled much since. There isn't enough space so we are crammed in like sardines, hundreds of sweaty bodies, most of whom haven't had a bath for some time. Others who couldn't get in are squeezed against the windows outside, stopping what little breeze there might be from entering. I wonder if I will faint. In any case, I can't see an easy way of leaving. 'Breathe deeply and slowly,' I tell myself, optimistically.

It is a pity I never learnt 'Wichi Thlamtes', the language these people speak. On the other hand, Alfredo's sermon doesn't seem too inspiring. He looks at his feet as he speaks, making eye contact with no one. He is scarcely audible, and I am near the front. I remember one of my colleagues, a linguist, speaking to this same man for about an hour outside our home one day. Afterwards, I asked him what they had talked about. 'Well,' said my colleague, 'I understood every word he said but I have no idea what he was on about.' The cultural gap between us seems like a chasm. The Wichi are not a demonstrative people, but this is extreme even by their standards. I sit as patiently as I can. It is only an hour now to midnight. Hopefully the service will end soon after and we can go to bed. He drones on for a very long time. Finally he sits down.

People do a bit of shuffling and jockeying for position, but there are no positions to jockey for. 'Health and safety in public buildings' has not yet arrived in Carboncito. There is another Bible reading, a song or two and then someone else gets up to speak. It's not very dazzling, but it is in Spanish, so at least I can understand it. Not long to go now. Nearly midnight!

Then we have a time of open thanksgiving. Several people from around the room chip in. Someone offers what sounds like a very animated prayer. There is a loud 'Amen.' Others join in, some in Wichi, some in Spanish. There is a definite change in mood. People stand up as they pray, and they do not sit down again afterwards. A woman starts to sing. We all join in. Now we are all on our feet. We begin to clap in time with the music. Then we begin to tap our feet, move our feet. 'In this heat we'll all faint,' I think. But actually, it suddenly seems cooler. There is a sort of refreshing breeze. I cannot see where it is coming from as the windows are even more blocked than before. It seems to be coming from inside us. Part of me is an astonished observer. Are these really the same reserved, stoic people I know?

The rejoicing is now in full swing. We are caught up in music, gladness, singing, laughter. Despite the lack of space we are all moving around, embracing one another. A very large woman grabs hold of me and gives me a huge hug. She is all boobs and sweat, and her scarf has half fallen off her head, but her face is alight with joy. 'Thank God,' she says. 'Thank God for his goodness.' A very small man comes to embrace me. He seems to disappear under my armpit. 'Praise God,' he is saying. 'He has delivered us and set us free.' I look at my watch. It is nearly 1 a.m. The tiredness has drained away. I feel refreshed, alive and full of energy, and so does everyone else. We dance on into the night.

> *Abbot Lot came to Abbot Joseph and said: 'Father, according as I am able I keep my little rule, and my little fast, my prayer, meditation and contemplative silence; and according as I am able I strive to cleanse my heart of evil thoughts: now what more should I do?' The elder rose up in reply and stretched out his hands to heaven, and his fingers blazed like ten lamps of fire. He said: 'Why not be totally changed into fire?'*
>
> Merton, 1970

Welcome

This is love, not that we loved God, but that He first loved us.

1 John 4.10

We thank you O Lord that you love us.

Prayer of a man in Soweto shortly after his house had been bulldozed by white South African troops, as reported by Desmond Tutu

Mike, a missionary with the Quakers (more specifically the 'North West Friends') has invited me to go with him to a remote part of the 'Altiplano' in Bolivia. It is over 15,000 feet above sea level and too high to grow anything much apart from the rough pasture on which the alpaca graze. The 'Friends' are keen to help introduce some vegetables into the diet and have developed a system of sunken greenhouses which heat up nicely during the day and retain much of the heat in the freezing-cold nights. The deal is that the local people dig the pits and build the adobe brick structures, and the mission provides the clear plastic roofing material (glass is soon broken by the inch-diameter hailstones). The tomatoes are not growing too well and I have been roped in as the nearest thing to a tomato expert to try and see why.

As always in these sorts of trips, we are delayed. We set off late from La Paz. The roofing materials aren't ready for loading, we have to make a diversion to drop someone off, we have a couple of punctures – all the usual stuff. We have no way of communicating with the village as there is neither phone nor electricity. It is miles from anywhere, near the Chilean border. As the sun goes down it becomes colder and colder. Mike is in his element and keeps stopping the truck to look at the stars which, with the high altitude and clear sky, form a dazzling canopy above us.

It is after midnight when we finally arrive. The village is in total darkness. All the houses are shut up for the night. No one stirs. 'We'll have to spend the night in the truck,' exclaims Mike cheerfully, clearly relishing the thought and getting out his telescope to observe the night sky more closely. Our breath is already freezing on the windscreen. I can only think about how cold I am and wonder if we will be discovered, frozen to our seats, in the morning.

Then a dim light appears in one of the huts. Then another. Doors open and people come out carrying torches and candles. I have never met these people before but they greet me like a long-lost friend, with warm handshakes and broad grins. 'Welcome! You are most welcome. We are very glad you've come. Thank you for coming! Praise God!' Within five minutes the whole village has got up and come out to greet us.

We are led to a small house where a fire is blown into life. We sit down to chat with some of the leaders. A crowd assembles around the door, laughing and joking. From somewhere else comes the smell of meat cooking. After a while we are presented with enough roasted alpaca to feed a whole family for a week. It is pretty tough but very tasty. It is now past 1 a.m. but we try our best to do it justice and invite others to join us. 'No,' they say; 'this is for you!' When we have finished they lead us to another hut where they have laid down two large piles of alpaca skins as beds, with some knitted alpaca blankets on top.

I am overwhelmed. I reflect on what sort of welcome unexpected visitors arriving late at night might expect at my home (even people I know and love, never mind the ones I've never met before!). I feel ashamed.

But it has also stirred up in me a picture. A picture of a God who is not stuck in heaven, enjoying life alone. Nor is God sitting there, distant and remote with arms folded, unconcerned about our plight. This is the God, to quote Carl Rahner, of 'venturesome love'. The God who is not static nor content to keep riches for personal pleasure. This is the God who cannot help but reach out, who longs for others to share the riches of his glory. The God who loves us with all his heart, all her soul, all his mind, all her strength. This is the God who rushes out to welcome us gladly, with open, outstretched arms. This is the God whose image I clearly saw, imprinted on the warm, smiling, weathered faces of Aymaran Indian villagers very late one night, miles from anywhere, near the Chilean border, in the bleak and freezing cold of the altiplano.

Footnote

This trip was definitely a one-way blessing, at least as far as I was concerned. The following morning, after breakfast, we set off walking across the icy wasteland to the place, just outside the village, where the greenhouses have been built. Mike and I, accompanied by a group of village 'elders', go down the steps into the first one. It is amazing how it has retained its warmth through the cold night. There are a number of crops, well advanced, but the main thing they have planted is tomatoes. I look at the plants. This is not a bush variety but they seem to have taken over one whole side of the greenhouse. There are some tomatoes ripening, but they are very small.

'Haven't you nipped out the laterals?' I ask.

A serious man at the front asks: 'What are laterals?'

'Well,' I reply, 'as the plant grows, it produces lots of side shoots between the leaves and the main stem. If you don't nip them out you will get masses of greenery, but not much in the way of a tomato crop.' They all nod gravely. I decide that a demonstration would be better than an explanation. Unfortunately, these bushes are already too far gone. It is impossible to work out which is the main stem and which are laterals. I look for a younger plant and spot a couple in the far bed.

'Look,' I go on, well into my stride by now. 'You see these small shoots here – and here. These are laterals. You need to nip them out as soon as they begin to develop.' As I demonstrate, some of the men at the back have their hands over their mouths. They are looking at their feet, scarcely suppressing laughter. One turns away with a snort.

The serious man at the front nods gravely. 'Those are potato plants,' he says.

Unwelcome

'Pastor, is there a place for me in your church?'

Question asked of Walter Wangerin Jnr by a black, unemployed, single parent in a very white, middle-class church in Chicago. The initial answer was 'Yes', but actually, it turned out to be 'No'.

A woman plucks up her courage, takes the baby in her arms and walks across Leeds to the church she has known and loved for some years. Her first child was baptized there. She used to worship there regularly and help out in the soup kitchen for homeless men. However, since they moved it is a bit far to walk, and, to be honest, with the oldest one now 3 she fears he might disturb people during the service. This is before the days of the crèche! Although she is not now a regular worshipper, faith remains important to her. She is a woman of strong moral values, someone who prays regularly. And this is 'her' church.

She does feel a bit nervous as she approaches the vestry door. 'Baptism and Wedding Enquiries 4–6 p.m. on Thursdays' says the notice. But it is not the same vicar she used to know, and she's never met the new one.

At last it is her turn. She takes a deep breath and walks in. The vicar sits behind the desk. 'Yes, what can I do for you?' he asks. She explains that they had the oldest one done here and now there's the youngest and she'd like him christened as well and wonders when would be a convenient time?

The vicar begins to write down the details. Date of birth? Child's surname and Christian names? Father's name? Occupation? Mother's name? Occupation? It all seems to be going OK.

Address? '14, Back Pleasant Dairies' she replies. 'Where's that?' asks the vicar. 'Oh, it's over the other side of Woodhouse Lane, off Blackman Lane,' she replies. He puts his pen down. 'Well, that's not in this parish at all,' he exclaims. 'Are you on the electoral roll?' It has never occurred to her to be on an electoral roll, whatever that is. 'I don't think so. I did used to come regular and I helped out in the crypt,' she says nervously. 'Well,' he says, tearing the form from the pad, ripping it in half and throwing it in the bin, 'You can't have him baptized here. You'll have to go to your own parish church – All Hallows, I think. Goodbye.'

Tears of anger and hurt well up as she turns to leave. She feels ashamed and stupid as she begins the long walk home. What will she tell her husband? Most of all she feels rejected by the church she loved, the church she tried her best to serve. It is a feeling that does not go away for many years to come.

I should know. She is my mother. I am the child in her arms.

Oh God, how could we have got it so badly wrong?
How could we have taken your open arms of love and
turned them into closed doors for so many people?

Mystery

Teenagers:
Tired of being harassed
by your stupid parents?
Act Now!!!
Move out, find a flat,
Get a job, pay your own bills,
While you still know everything.

Popular poster

When I was 21 I did know everything. For example, I was an excellent parent and deeply critical of how others brought up their children (that was before I had any actual children of my own!). In matters of faith and doctrine I had all the 'i's dotted and all the 't's crossed! In fact it could all be reduced to four clear points which were contained in a booklet I kept handy in my pocket to share with unconsenting adults.

But now it's the summer holidays and we are off hitch-hiking around France, northern Italy and Switzerland for three weeks. A month before we set off we are at a party. A bloke we've never met asks us where we are going on holiday. 'Ah,' he exclaims, 'you must go to Taizé.' 'Taizé?' we ask. 'What's that?'

He begins to tell us about this remarkable community in the middle of France which began, after the war, to develop into a place of reconciliation. Astonishingly, without any advertising, young people started to turn up from all over France. Then they began to come from other parts of Europe and, indeed, the world.

'What happens there?' we ask. 'Well, why don't you go and see?' he replies. It turns out to be pretty much 'en route' so we decide to check it out.

Hitching turns out to be difficult. The week before we arrive in France a motorist is killed by a hitch-hiker, so the going is slow. We finally arrive at Taizé, glad of somewhere we can pitch our tent and get off the road for a day or two. We are astonished to find the whole place teeming with teenagers and young adults. There seem to be several thousand milling around. We sign in, pitch the tent and turn up for a bowl of aubergine stew. Then it's time for the evening service. The church, a modern building, holds a couple of thousand people. However, they have just knocked down the back wall in order to extend it. We squeeze in and sit down.

The songs are simple and very repetitive. We soon pick them up. There are a lot of candles and 'icons' knocking about which seem pretty dodgy to us. Brother Roger preaches. It does not seem to be anything like what we've been used to. He doesn't stick closely to the Bible text we've just heard read. It certainly doesn't coincide with what's written in the booklet in my pocket. We go to some of the discussion groups and finally talk to one of the 'brothers'. 'What is going on?' we ask. We feel confused. This does not seem to be the gospel message we have been so certain about at all. And all these young people knocking about? No one is socking the gospel to them. What a wasted opportunity!

We are not sure we can put our fingers on what it is we are experiencing. It is not so much a different booklet as a coming into contact with things which cannot be tied down or defined at all. We are not at all sure this is 'sound' – but as we walk into the worship, there is a mysterious, overwhelming sense of God's presence and power which we simply cannot deny. And thousands of young people from across Europe, many alienated from their churches back home, are finding it too. Here they feel they belong – the first great step in evangelism, according to Archbishop William Temple. 'Belonging, believing and behaving', in that order. Here they are encountering Christ.

All I can think of is the passage from St John's Gospel: 'The wind of the Spirit blows wherever it chooses. You can hear the sound of it, see the effects, but you've no idea where it's coming from or where it will go next.'

For the first time, I begin to wonder if I *do* know everything, after all?

> *'Tis mystery all, the Saviour dies*
> *Who can explore his strange design?*
>
> Charles Wesley

Community

There is no such thing as society.

Margaret Thatcher

It is the harvest season. There will not be much sleep for the next few weeks as we seek to harvest, pack and, finally, transport the tomatoes, peppers and runner beans from the community farms in the Chaco to the markets in Buenos Aires, over 1,000 miles away. Transport is by open, un-refrigerated truck over some pretty bad roads. Speed is of the essence. Too long in the sweltering, desert heat of Santiago del Estero, and what arrives at market is little better than tomato sauce!

Arturo is the key to all this. He organizes the transport. He is one of the lads. What you might call 'a diamond geezer'. A mover. He needs to be, since the radio at his house is constantly buzzing with messages from the markets, from the lorries in transit and from 30 or 40 different farms to say they've got 50 or maybe 600 boxes of tomatoes that need to go *now!* In the summer he can relax, watch football, barbeque a huge pile of beef, enjoy his seven children and a drink at the bar. But not now. I don't know when he finds time to sleep.

It is 2.30 p.m. Everything is closed until 4 p.m. People are in bed enjoying a siesta. The small town we live in has ground to a halt – except for Arturo. He has just been on the radio and now he's got to drive 15 miles to check the load at a farm before meeting the incoming empty lorries and allocating them a cargo. He rushes out of the house and jumps into his pickup. He starts the engine and roars off. There is a strange bump.

First the front wheel and then the back. Better have a look. He jumps out of the cab and round to the near side.

There, under the back wheel, is the still, crushed body of Enrique, his 2-year-old son, who has been asleep under the front wheel in the shade. A crimson stream flows into the gutter.

The whole town is in shock. People come to their home where the tiny, open coffin sits on the living-room table. There is nothing that can be said that is of any comfort at all. Arturo takes Enrique's hand and weeps out loud as he pleads: '*Why? Why?*'

The funeral is the following morning. In the hot climate, with no refrigerated morgue, it cannot be delayed. The coffin is carried on the back of the same deadly pickup. The family walk behind, slowly making their way across town to the church, and then the cemetery. As they come around the first bend people close up their houses and come outside to meet them. There are now a hundred or more people walking behind the truck. Shops shut, garages close down, shutters are lowered, children in school stop their work and are silent. Everything grinds to a halt – except the funeral procession which has now swelled to over a thousand people. As we approach the central 'Plaza' over half the town are following on behind the battered truck with its tiny cargo.

In turn, people move forward to take Arturo's arm. Some say a few words. Most say nothing. They simply hold him and his family in their strong embrace. After a short while they drop back, allowing others to come forward and take their place, like an endless chain, bearing them along the dirt roads.

The walk to the church takes an hour. Then there is another half-hour to the cemetery. But no one is thinking of leaving them to make it alone. A remote border town with little to commend it is taking its stance today. It is proclaiming, far louder than words, that this family will not stand alone. There is a community here. There is solidarity. Arturo's family have descended into the most terrible tragedy. There are many dark days to come still. They are broken, fallen. But they will not fall alone. They will be borne up by others, lifted back to life.

> *Two are better than one . . . for if they fall, they can help each other up, but woe to the one who falls alone . . .*
> *A threefold cord is even better. It proves hard to break.*
>
> Ecclesiastes 4.9–12

II

Incarnation

I bind this day to me for ever
By power of faith
Christ's Incarnation.

From 'St Patrick's Breastplate'

A word of introduction . . .

And the Word became flesh and blood
And lived among us
Full of grace and truth.

From John 1.14

Much of this book is about the Incarnation and its consequences. Literally, incarnation means 'in the flesh'. It is about God the Son emptying himself of the glory of heaven and taking the risk to be born, not to aristocracy in a palace, but to an ordinary working-class couple from Nazareth.

Having babies is very much an 'in the flesh' experience. Once the initial glow has worn off, it's down to the real business. Waking up to the crying in the middle of the night, getting up to feed, finding the excess regurgitated all over your shoulder as you attempt to induce belching. Hearing the squidge from below just after you've changed him, which has not only leaked on to the babygrow but also through onto your shirt. Then, sluicing the terry nappy down the loo, avoiding splash-back and trying not to let go. (What *are* the current generation of Western parents missing with disposable nappies?) Incarnation is very definitely 'in the flesh'.

In Jesus, God faces all the joys and frustrations, all the dangers and difficulties which life can hold. He is born in a dirty cowshed far away from his parents' home. His parents flee for their lives as refugees to avoid infanticide. He knows what it's like to play with his mates, fall over, cut his leg and run home crying to his mum. He faces, in all probability, the painful early death of his father and takes on the family carpentry business. He goes to parties, eats, drinks and has a laugh. He studies the Bible and talks politics. He faces the stigma of illegitimacy from those who have no inkling of his divine origin. '*We're* not bastards! We know who *our* Father is – God himself!' taunt the Jewish leaders (John 8.41). He gets angry, grows weary, weeps, feels afraid.

As he grows up he begins to realize who he is, discovers what it is to be 'one with the Father', always looking to spend time alone with him in prayer. He discovers the power of the Spirit inside him, at work through his healing hands and his astonishing words of authority and grace. He walks in our shoes, shares our sorrows and our joys, knows what it's like to be in our place. He shows us how to live – not as one who sets rules he has no intention of keeping himself, but as one who has been there, who says to us 'Come on, I've lived your life so that you can share mine.' He brings God down to earth, so that men and women can find their way back to God, for ever.

He is Emmanuel – God with us. For as is Jesus Christ, so is God. There is no different God in heaven. If we want to know what the Father and the Spirit are like, they are exactly like the Son. 'But now God has spoken to us through his Son,' says the writer to the Jewish Christians. 'He is the one who reflects God's own glory. He is the exact likeness of God's own being' (Hebrews 1.2, 3). He is one of us. Yet he is unique. He is God.

He lived among us in flesh and blood for about 30 years on earth. And, through his ascension into heaven, he takes for ever our humanity into the heart of God. Through the Holy Spirit he is present with us in the world, here and now, in the most unlikely people, in the most unexpected places. After all, how else would we meet him?

> *'I tell you the truth,' said Jesus. 'Whatever you did to the least of these brothers and sisters of mine, you did it to me.'*
>
> From Matthew 25

Unlikely Choice

Treat everyone equally. Don't be a snob, but make real friends with those who are poor.

Romans 12.16

I am sitting at my desk planning the service for Mothering Sunday. It is a big 'do'. The uniformed organizations will be there and, for reasons I do not quite understand, it is one of those times of year when people come to church. We have organized flowers for the mums, the Sunday Club are doing a slot, the music is sorted, my colleague is doing the all-age address, and everything is falling into place. Then the phone goes.

'Oh, hello Alan, it's Norma. You know our Scott is coming with the Cubs on Sunday? Well, he's singing a solo in the school production of the *Jungle Book* called "My own mother". Wouldn't it be marvellous if he sang it in church on Sunday?'

My heart begins to sink. The service already looks as if it may be longer than I had hoped. I ask if she can read me the lyrics. As I suspected, it is not exactly a biblical message. On the other hand, I don't want to discourage people from participating. I have a sneaky feeling I might regret this. Scott is a special-needs kid from a broken home who, as far as I know, has never done any solo singing before. Ah well, here goes nothing. 'Yes,' I say, with a very large pinch of 'No'; 'that would be lovely.'

But that week something happens that makes me rue the decision even more. On the morning of Wednesday 13 March 1996, a man with a gun breaks into the infants' school in

Dunblane and shoots dead 16 children and a teacher. It is tragedy of terrible proportions that sends shock-waves around the whole nation. It will certainly be the main thing on everyone's mind on Mother's Day, as all those mothers and fathers in Dunblane will be in the pit of bitter anguish and grief, instead of a family celebration.

I try and think about how we can reflect this tragedy in our service. Obviously, in our prayers. We also make a huge card with a picture of a single candle burning in the darkness, which we plan to get everyone to sign before sending it off to Scotland. It does not seem the moment to be having a song from the *Jungle Book* in mid-service. However, since it was arranged there have been three more excited phone calls from Norma about the great event. Even Scott's dedicated music teacher from school has offered to come and play the piano for him! There is no going back. I grit my teeth, say a prayer and hope for the best.

Because of the tragedy even more people than normal turn up for the service. There is a sombre mood. It seems to be going OK but I feel we haven't quite captured the moment. We are three-quarters of the way through the service now and my colleague is next up to do the address; after, that is, Scott's solo.

He stands up and walks to the front. He stands to attention in his Cubs uniform, looking nervous. I can see his legs shaking. The teacher begins to play. He holds his head up and starts to sing.

I do not remember the words at all. What I remember is Scott, this unlikely lad, singing with such passion, such emotion, such tenderness, such power and conviction, and with a haunting clarity and depth, that everybody weeps. We are suddenly released from all the anxiety of not knowing how to respond or what to say and caught up in the pain and anguish of the moment. It is as though, for an instant at least, God had brought us to the foot of the cross, that place of desolation where, with the people of Dunblane, we stand and weep.

Of course, the Bible is full of these unlikely characters who turn out to be the vessels God works through in a most astonishing way. Jacob, a real toe-rag if ever there was one, who becomes the father of Israel. Moses, the murdering coward with a stutter, whom God sends back, when he is already an old man, to lead his people from slavery to freedom. David, the youngest son of Jesse, too unimportant to call in from the fields when the mighty prophet Samuel arrives, but who becomes the greatest king in Israel's history.

And now Mary, a nobody – and a northerner to boot – a most unlikely choice to become the mother of God's only Son.

Mary sang:

'My heart proclaims the greatness of the Lord
My spirit rejoices in God my Saviour
For he has noticed me, a serving girl.
From now on people throughout history will call me "Blessed".
He has swept away the proud and dashed their plans
And thrown rulers from their thrones.
But he has lifted up nobodies
And given the hungry their fill of good things
While the rich are turned away empty-handed.'

From the 'Magnificat', Luke 1

Saying 'Yes'

Jesus Christ, the Son of God, whom we have proclaimed to you, is not some doubtful 'Yes and No'. With Him it is always 'Yes!' Indeed every single one of God's promises finds its 'Yes' in Him.

2 Corinthians 1.19, 20

Rob and Jenny are a great couple. I have known them for their last two years at university. They have been preparing for the big day for a long time, and now it has arrived. Rob has been here with the best man for over half an hour. He is a bit nervous but his enthusiasm is infectious. He has been engaged before, some time ago. When his previous fiancée broke it off he was devastated. But a year or so later he met Jenny. Surely nothing can go wrong this time?

The church fills up and, eventually, Jenny arrives, escorted down the aisle by her proud dad. She looks lovely. I welcome people, there is a short introduction. We sing a hymn. Now down to the real business.

I read out the purpose of Christian marriage. I then remind the congregation that they are not only 'here for the beer'. They are Rob and Jenny's closest family and friends. It's not easy to make a marriage work these days. Rob and Jenny will need their love and support for years to come. 'Are you willing to give it to them?' I ask. 'We are,' comes the reply. Now we need to enquire if anyone has a reason in law why they may not be married. There is an awkward silence. I wonder how I would handle it if someone did stand up and object. Luckily, no one does. A small sigh of relief. Now for the vows. I turn to Rob.

Before I can say anything he has set off like a steam train. In a loud voice he begins: 'I Rob take you Jenny to be my wife, to have and to hold, from this day forward, for better for worse, for richer for poorer, in sickness and in health . . . ' He has learned them off by heart.

I butt in. 'Hang on, Rob,' I say. 'I know you're keen. But we haven't got to that bit yet!'

There is a wave of laughter around the church. People visibly relax. Rob laughs and looks at Jenny. She squeezes his hand. (I often wonder if I should include a deliberate mistake in the early stages of a wedding. If you handle it well, it seems to wash away all the tension.)

We go on with the service. Rob has to makes his promises to God before he makes them to Jenny. 'Rob,' I ask him, 'will you take Jenny to be your lawful wedded wife? Will you love her and comfort her, honour and protect her and, forsaking all others, be faithful to her alone as long as you both shall live?'

'*I will*,' he affirms. Jenny says the same. Then they turn to each other.

'Now Rob,' I say, 'this is the moment.' He takes her hand in his and recites perfectly the vows he has learned with his mind and longs to keep with his whole heart. Then it's Jenny's turn. She looks straight at him and says her vows with conviction. They exchange rings and I proclaim them to be husband and wife.

'That which God has joined together let no one separate.'

They walk down the aisle with a spring in their step, to be met by a hail of confetti and flashing cameras at the door.

He has not been rejected this time. She loves him, and she has said yes!

I sometimes wonder if God's first choice may have been a Judith or a Deborah or a Miriam? It would not have been the first time God was rejected in love.

Whatever the case, Mary, like Jenny, said yes.

> *'I am God's servant,' says Mary, 'may it be to me exactly as you have said.'*
>
> Luke 1.38

Christmas Morning

A God who is squeaky clean in a dirty universe is – surely – not properly God.

Hinksman, 1999

At 8.30 a.m. on 27 December I walk round the corner to the local 'Spar' for some milk. I join the queue of early-morning shoppers who are suffering 'withdrawal symptoms' after two days without shopping.

'Morning Margaret,' I say, to the lady next to me in the queue. 'Had a good Christmas?'

'No we haven't!' she says with conviction. 'I hope we never have another one like it!' She begins to tell me about it.

The preparations all went pretty well. They have been saving up for ages for the stuff the kids wanted – paying into a club. They've even managed a few little extras. Rick's parents are coming down from Liverpool to stay for a few days. That has been a source of friction in the past, but they arrive on Christmas Eve and everything seems to be going smoothly. By 10.30 p.m. the kids are all shipped off to bed with strict instructions that no one is allowed down before 6.30 a.m.! The adults enjoy a drink and a bit of TV. The presents are piled up under the tree in the window. The lights twinkle. It all looks magic.

But at 6.15 a.m. Margaret and Rick have a rude awakening. There is a sound of shouting, screaming and crying from downstairs. Then the three older children rush into their bedroom. 'You'll never guess what Jack's done,' they blurt out, faces flushed with angry tears. Jack, the youngest, is still downstairs. They can hear him crying on his own.

Jack has woken early with all the excitement. He wanders down to the living-room on his own at the crack of dawn. He can't tell the time yet, so whatever '6.30 a.m.' means, it must be now. Unfortunately he can't read either. So how is he supposed to know which presents are his? He rips the wrapping paper off one near the top. It's something in a box. He opens the box. A radio sort of thing. That can't be his. He throws it to one side and grabs the next one. It's a Barbie doll with a horse. He fiddles with it for a while and then puts it to one side. That must be for his sister. Next up is a small packet with a bottle of something in it. He unscrews the top. Cor, it doesn't half smell. He tries to put the top back on. Not so easy. Some of it spills on the carpet. Never mind. Must be for Grandma. She always smells like that. He puts it by the fire. Maybe he should wait for the others to come? Well, one more. Mmmmm. A selection box. He opens it up and chooses a big bag of 'Chocolate Buttons'. They are hard to open and when they do they seem to fly everywhere. He eats a few, then half a Mars bar. Time to start unwrapping again. More tricky now as his hands are covered in chocolate and things seem a bit more slippery. A book. He flicks through it with his chocolatey hands. No pictures. He tosses it to one side and picks up another parcel. He is well into his stride.

When the others come down, about two hours later, Jack is in the corner, playing with Robbie's 'Action Man'. The living-room reeks of aftershave and eau de Cologne. There is a huge pile of torn-up wrapping paper. Presents are strewn across the floor, smeared in chocolate. Every single one has been opened. It is a complete mess – and so is the rest of Christmas for Margaret and her family.

Actually, the first Christmas was not all that great either. A long journey on foot in the final stages of pregnancy to a strange town. You are not yet married and the man you are engaged to isn't the child's father. Then when you arrive, far from home, there is nowhere to stay so you end up in a smelly cowshed with only Joseph around to help with the birth and mop up the blood.

And it is there, in the mess, in the midst of torn paper, melted chocolate and spilled perfume, in the tears of anger, disappointment and regret, that Christ comes to us, just as we are.

When the time was right God sent the Son.
Lover of the unloveable, toucher of the untouchable,
forgiver of the unforgiveable,
bone of our bone, flesh of our flesh,
writing heaven's pardon over earth's mistakes.
The Word became flesh, He lived among us, He was one of us.

From the Iona Community Worship Book

Christmas

O Holy Child of Bethlehem,
descend to us we pray:
cast out our sin and enter in,
be born in us today.

Traditional carol

It is Christmas Day at last. The long round of carol concerts, assemblies, Christmas Fayres, special lunches, Christingles, candlelit services and children's parties is over. It's been a good couple of weeks but now I am really exhausted and desperate for a break. At last we are sitting around the table, just the family, about to serve second helpings of turkey and looking forward to a relaxing week in front of the fire and the box.

The doorbell goes. Oh no! It can't be. Surely not now of all moments? Not in the middle of Christmas dinner. Doesn't she have any respect?

The long, sustained note tells me at once that it's Flora. Flora used to have a decent job in an office. But then there were scratch cards: and now she's hooked. She trails from door to door, in her daily round across the parish. She asks for £1.50, £1, then 50p. No? OK then, do I have any milk, orange squash, cigars, bread? No one has her pension book and handbag stolen more often in a week than Flora! What she really wants is the money for the scratch card – the next one might just be the winner – but she'll settle for the food, which she may be able to sell down the road for cash.

At the fourth ring I get up reluctantly and grudgingly and go to the door.

'Yes Flora, what do you want this time?'

'Oh,' she says, 'nothing.' She smiles a broad toothless grin and hands me a box of Marks and Spencer chocolates. 'Happy Christmas,' she says as she turns and waddles off down the path.

I stare down the path long after she is gone, reflecting on my ungracious welcome and mean spirit. And, despite the tiredness, Christ is born in me again.

Temptation

The essential message of the book of Job is this: 'is it possible to serve God for no reward?'

Gustavo Gutierrez, Divinity School Cambridge, 1991

Then the Holy Spirit led Jesus into the desert where, for forty days, he was tempted by the devil.

'If you are the Son of God, why do without? Turn these stones into whatever you fancy.'

'If you are the Son of God, throw yourself off the Temple – that would make them sit up and take notice of you!'

'OK. Let's be straight. Just throw your lot in with me and the world's your oyster!'

See Matthew 4

On a good day, with the sun in your face and the wind at your back, being a vicar is a great job. I'm my own boss; I work flexi-time; I meet a lot of different people; I love doing stuff with the kids at church and in the local schools; it gives me freedom to work and to speak out on all the issues I feel passionately about; it is a great privilege to be involved in people's lives at crucial moments, to share their sorrows and their joys, to see God at work. There is even a lot of satisfaction in doing a decent funeral. And anyway, it's what I feel called to. It *is* a great job, and most of them are indeed 'good days'.

But today is not one of them. Another hole in the fence! More hassle – and as soon as we get it fixed the kids will bust it again to restore the short cut into the community centre. One of the hall users has just been round to complain that the heating has failed (again) and that chairs were left all over the hall. Some people are so petty. Couldn't she have moved them? Does she think I've nothing better to do than move chairs and ring insurance companies? It's OK if you are in a big church with several staff to handle it, but that's not us. Even worse, three of our most committed members have just moved away from Cambridge, so we've even fewer people to do the work.

And to cap it all, an already busy week has had to accommodate two funerals. That has thrown everything else, and I'm way behind on preparation and visiting. I sit at my desk trying to get ready for tonight's United Lent Study Group, resenting the time, knowing that, despite what they have said, there'll probably only be a handful of people there. I reflect on the way I've handled the unity issue. I fear that I've been so keen to press forward that others have seen me as 'pushy' and it's had the effect of making them more wary. It would be good to talk to somebody in the diocese about it. Trouble with the Church of England is there's no middle management, no one to touch base with every couple of weeks or so. Our bishops and archdeacons are good people, but I hardly ever see them. And, in any case, they're so busy I don't like calling them unless it's an emergency. Of course, they'd soon be round if I ran off with the church secretary or fiddled the books! Or maybe they wouldn't even notice? I wonder if they have any idea what goes on here from week to week? It would be nice, just occasionally, to get a bit of recognition, a bit of thanks.

I'll have to cycle to the meeting tonight with arms full of stuff – Annie needs the car. If I were still a Chemical Engineer we'd have at least two cars! I wonder how much I'd be earning now? I'd probably be a senior manager with some real clout . . .

Personal fulfilment; recognition; power. The same old three. I hear again the straightforward call: 'Take up your cross, every day, and follow me.'

Tomorrow I will stop feeling sorry for myself and get on with it.

I struck the board and cry'd: 'No More!'
I will abroad.
Have I no harvest but a thorn?

But as I raved and grew more fierce and wilde
At every word,
Me thoughts I heard one calling, 'Child':
And I reply'd: 'My Lord'.

From 'The Collar' by George Herbert

I am no longer mine but yours,
Put me to what you will, rank me with whom you will;
Let me be employed for you, let me be laid aside for you;
Let me be exalted for you, let me be brought low for you;
I freely and wholeheartedly yield everything to your pleasure and disposal.

From John Wesley's Covenant Prayer

Prayer

Very early in the morning, while it was still dark, Jesus got up and went off to find an isolated place, on his own, to pray.

Mark 1.35

It is my first time on silent retreat, alone. I wonder how I will cope, how I will get through the days with no one to talk to and no TV. I am not someone who has a natural burning desire to pray. And I certainly don't have a lot of self-discipline, either.

What is it about prayer that seems to be so essential for some people? I think of the funeral I went to a while ago in Birmingham. Brenda was an elderly woman who had never married, never had children. She left school at 14 and worked all her life on the production line at Cadbury's chocolate factory. She wasn't involved in politics, didn't sit on committees, never had much money.

But the church is packed for her funeral. She is a nobody, and yet over 500 people have turned up to see her off. Her home was always open, with a cuppa on the go and a listening ear. And she certainly never forgot us in her prayers despite not seeing us for years on end.

I think of another encounter, in this same church, on our wedding day some years earlier. I am down here early to check on the caterers who are preparing the buffet in the church hall. A woman in her 40s is having a look round. I get chatting to her. It turns out she has come for our wedding that afternoon. She is my future wife's aunt, not someone I've met before.

As we chat it becomes plain to her that Christian faith is pretty important to us. She looks at me with tears in her eyes. 'Actually,' she says, 'I'm Annie's godmother. I haven't seen much of her over the years, but I have prayed for her every day since she was born.'

The vicar referred to Brenda in his funeral address as a 'Mighty prayer warrior.' So she was. So were they both.

I wonder what difference it makes. A useless waste of time in a world of activity? Or is it the place where we can get back in touch with the Father's love, bring to God all the stuff in our hearts, wrestle with the difficult issues inside and around us, regain strength for the difficult days to come, find a new perspective for the way ahead? Certainly for Jesus it was the vital substance of life. He just had to do it.

I get back to the business and think of the disciples, who obviously felt a bit like me as they saw Jesus coming back from yet another prayer session on his own (Luke 11.1).

'Lord, teach us how to pray.'

'Lord, teach me *how to pray.'*

Only One Body

Very early in the morning, while it was still dark, Jesus got up quietly and went off on his own to a remote place to pray. Later on, Simon and the others saw he was gone and went out looking for him. When they found him they said: 'Where've you been? Everyone is desperate to see you.' But Jesus said: 'Come on, let's go. We can't just stay here. We need to go and tell the Good News to all the neighbouring towns as well. That's the whole purpose of me coming.'

Mark 1.35–8

I am on my way to the post office. A neighbour greets me in the street. We talk about the weather, the community café, why the council can't manage to run a bus service to the hospital – all the usual stuff. She makes to walk on, then hesitates and says: 'Oh, by the way, Mr Johnson, you know, number 47, he's not too good. Be nice if you could pop in and see him, when you've got the time.' And off she goes.

I make a note in my diary under 'visits'. This week is pretty full. I'll go next week. Next week turns out to be just as full. The following Wednesday afternoon looks OK. I'll definitely go then. No rush. Mr Johnson has been 'not too good' for some time.

On Tuesday morning the phone rings. 'Hello. Co-op Funeral Service. We'd like to arrange the funeral of the late Mr Johnson – lived just down the road from you didn't he?'

Being human is painful. There never is enough time. 'If only there were 40 hours in a day.' But it still wouldn't be enough.

And Christ felt the dilemma just as acutely as we do. It's been a heavy day's ministry. The disciples are exhausted. When they finally hit the sack they go out like a light. Another big day tomorrow. There'll be loads of people who didn't get to see Jesus today queuing up first thing. Not sure if he'll get round them all tomorrow either. But he doesn't even try. He gets up in the early hours while the rest are asleep and clears off. When the disciples finally catch up with him they are pretty cheesed off. 'What are you messing at?' they say. 'Don't you realize everybody is out searching for you?' (Mark 1.35ff).

But, Jesus' ministry is not just to Capernaum. He can only be in one place at a time. Incarnation means accepting your limitations in the face of a very big crowd with high expectations. Even Jesus, limited in time and space to one human body, can't meet them all. So what he does has to be strategic. Yes, it is painful to leave behind all those people in the village. Yes, they will be bitterly disappointed. Yes, some of them are dying. But he's only got three more years. He's got to get around to as many towns and villages as possible. And then Jerusalem. He can't be diverted. He really has to make it count.

I have to make it count as well. I only have one life. I can't do everything. I have to spend my time on the things that really matter. The things that *will* make a difference. The things God has called me to do. It's the choosing *not* to do which is so painful. The needs are like a bottomless pit and, in any case, I don't always get it right.

Why, O why didn't I go and visit Mr Johnson, while there was still time?

Walking

Jesus walked through all the towns and villages, teaching in the synagogues, proclaiming the Good News of God's Kingdom and healing everyone who was ill.

Matthew 9.35

There are no short cuts to any place worth going to.

Beverley Sills

It is day three and I think I am going to have to give up. I have never had a go at a long-distance walk before. On previous walking holidays you could always decide, if it were raining or you were still tired after the previous day's exertion, to choose a short, valley walk, or visit a castle instead. But now we are committed to a route, we've got to carry all our stuff on our backs and the accommodation is all booked between Edale and Middleton-in-Teesdale.

I had wondered whether I'd have the stamina for it. I've planned it carefully and we're only doing 12–15 miles a day, with every fourth day off. But stamina is not the problem. Joints are the problem.

Nowadays you don't get stuck up to your knees in bog going over Kinder Scout. There is a pathway of granite slabs, dropped in by helicopter to protect the peat. It seems great at first but the pounding on your feet, your knees, your hips, especially going downhill, starts to become almost unbearable. By the time we reach Hebden Bridge I'm not sure I can continue.

However, after a trip to the chemist to dose up on ibuprofen and purchase various knee and ankle supports, plus a lightweight, adjustable aluminium walking-stick with a selection of tips for different types of path, we set off with renewed hope. By day six my body is still complaining, but I begin to believe it might just be possible.

Then something else starts to happen. I have heard people talk about having 'out-of-body' experiences. I've never had one myself but, as I walk along, I wonder if most of my life is like an out-of-body experience. I think of myself, a week last Wednesday. My body is sitting at my desk. My mind is still down the street, with the woman I've just visited who is undergoing chemotherapy. My spirit seems to be like an empty tank somewhere else, awaiting a refill. I am on auto-pilot.

But now, as I walk along the ridge, I can feel them coming together. Gradually my body, mind and spirit are all being integrated back into the present moment. All of me, the whole person, has been put back together and is proceeding down the Pennine Way at 2½ miles an hour.

I cannot help thinking of Jesus' ministry. Going everywhere on foot. Proceeding from place to place at walking speed. Allowing time to talk with people on the way. Gradually moving from place to place at a pace which allows interaction, conversation, listening, reflection, healing, love.

So very difficult to do in the car, lap-top and mobile phone culture. I wonder what we have lost; I wonder if we can find it again?

Dear God, we pray for another way of being: another way of knowing. Across the difficult terrain of our existence we have attempted to build a highway and in so doing have lost the footpath. Lead us to our footpath.
Nothing can be loved at speed.
God lead us to the slow path; to the joyous insights of the pilgrim; another way of knowing; another way of being.
Amen.

Leunig, 1993

Growth

Jesus told them this story: 'A farmer went out to sow. As he sowed, some seed fell on the path, where the birds quickly ate it up. Some fell on stony ground. It soon shot up but, because there was not much soil for its roots, when the sun grew hot it withered and died. Some seed fell among thorns, which grew up and choked it, so that it never produced any grain.'

From Mark 4

Moving into a new house is a challenge. This one was only built a couple of years ago and has been lived in by students who were 'house sitting' until the new vicar was appointed. We have the chance really to make it our own – particularly in the garden. However, it has been nobody's job to care for the garden this past couple of years, so nobody did. It will be a lot of hard work, but great to see it gradually taking shape.

But what about that small triangle of weeds outside the fence by the drive entrance? Yes! A group of slow-growing conifers will fill it nicely over the next few years, without much maintenance work. The family are less sure. It is a bit of a thoroughfare for local kids who run up our drive, climb over the wall and through the gap in the fence into the community centre. However, the following weekend I dig some holes, fill them with compost, plant the dozen conifers I've just bought and water them in. I stand back, well satisfied with my day's work.

Three weeks later I walk out of the front gate and six of the conifers have gone. I look around to see if kids have flung them over the hedge. No sign of them. It doesn't look like kids. They have been dug up. Someone has nicked them in the night.

My family are not surprised. They are sympathetic, of course, but nothing can hide that 'I told you so' look in their eyes.

'Why not just grass it over?' says my son. But something inside wants to prove them wrong. I go out and buy another half-dozen conifers.

They do OK for a while. One thing I hadn't banked on is that our drive is a convenient point for cars to reverse into and turn around, to save the long drive round the block to the main road. They don't always manage to hit the tarmac. The conifers near the edge have large tyre marks over the top of them. I replace them with a low-growing, spreading variety. They still get run over but, apart from one or two broken branches, seem to survive.

One morning, three months later, another five conifers have gone. 'Just give up, Dad,' says my daughter, seeing how upset I am by such a trivial thing. But it has become more than trivial: it has become a metaphor for my work here. Can I persevere, keep on planting, even when it looks hopeless?

I think of all the 'planting' parables Jesus told. I hadn't realized before how stupid the sower was in that parable. Fancy throwing all that good seed on the path, on the stony ground, in the weed patch. No chance! Why not just plant it all in the good soil? Isn't that the obvious plan? Maybe it's because he's really a carpenter and has no idea about farming?

But year after year he perseveres, hoping and praying, wanting to give every bit of ground a chance, longing that, one day, there will be a response, even in the most unlikely of places, to the seed of God's love and grace.

The following day I go out and buy five more conifers.

But some seed did fall on good soil, and it grew strong and produced grain, thirty, sixty and even a hundred times more than was planted.

The Way

I said to the man at the gate of the year: 'Give me a light that I may tread safely into the unknown.' And he replied: 'Go out into the darkness and put your hand into the hand of God. That shall be to you better than any light and safer than a known way.'

Minnie Haskins
(quoted by George VI in his Christmas message, 1939)

We have been living with Grandma and Granddad for several months. Leaving them for another three years to go back to South America is not going to be easy for any of us, especially for our 5-year-old who has made their home very much her own.

Our return does not start well. We are on our way to Bolivia but the first stop is Lima, Peru. We arrive at night and, due to a mix-up, there is no one to meet us at the airport. We sit the exhausted children on a pile of luggage and try to fend off the crowd of insistent bag-carriers and taxi drivers. Eventually we make it to our friends' house but our daughter is clearly unhappy. 'I don't like it here. I want to go back to Grandma's,' she says with a will.

I can understand her feelings. Lima, Peru is not most people's idea of paradise. The locals refer to it as the 'Inca's revenge'. The story goes that the Spanish Conquistadores asked the Incas where would be a good place to build their capital city. The Incas showed them Lima, knowing full well its horrible climate – a semi-desert where it never rains but is hot and humid with a sort of miserable sea-fog. As a result the streets are dirty, never washed with a good downpour, and many of the houses are only half-finished (why bother paying for a proper roof if it doesn't rain?).

But this is about more than just the place. Over the next few days our daughter talks of nothing but going home. She is not emotional, but she has made her mind up. She is going back to Grandma and Granddad's, and that is it. One morning I go up to her room and discover, to my dismay, that she has packed her bag. 'What are you doing?' I ask. 'I'm leaving this horrible place and going home!' she exclaims. Her voice is absolutely firm and her chin set like stone.

I go downstairs and talk to my wife. We are concerned that she may just go out of the front gate and wander off. As we talk she comes downstairs with her rucksack on her back and heads for the door. We try and tell her that it just isn't possible to go back to England, that we are thousands of miles away. But there is no reasoning with her.

'Right,' she says. 'I'm going' – and she walks out of the door. I look at my wife and decide there is only one thing to do. 'OK,' I say, 'I'll come with you' – and off we set.

We open the front gate. 'Which way?' I ask. 'Left,' she replies, without hesitation. We walk together to the end of the block. 'Which way now?' 'Straight on.' We cross the road and walk another block. 'Left again,' she proclaims without a trace of uncertainty. Another block. 'Right.' Another. 'Straight on.' We walk briskly on. 'Left', 'Left', 'Straight on', 'Right', 'Straight on.' But after a while the pace starts to slow and her hand grips mine a little more tightly.

After quite some time we arrive at yet another corner. 'Which way?' I ask gently. Her lip begins to quiver and she looks down at the floor. 'I don't know,' she says, and bursts into tears. I kneel down beside her on the path and hug her very tight. Several passers-by look at us, concerned. We are both weeping profusely. A woman asks if we are OK. I say yes, we're fine, though clearly we are not. After a few minutes we get up and walk slowly back to our friends' house. Tomorrow we leave for our new life in Bolivia.

We have lost our way. After a lot of struggle, over the next few weeks and months, we will find it again. But it will not involve a journey back to England, or anywhere else for that matter.

> *Jesus said: 'I am the way, the Truth and the Life. The only way you can get back home to the Father, is through me.'*
>
> John 14.6

Lost

God doesn't want anybody to be lost, but wants every single one to come safely home to Him.

2 Peter 3.9

It is a bright and sunny day, the kids are on holiday and there is great excitement. We are going to the zoo!

Santa Cruz has an excellent zoo. All the animals and birds are from Bolivia, which makes it particularly interesting. We are going with our friends, who also have four children. And there are a couple of other kids coming too. Fortunately the Watsons have a mini-bus and we can all squeeze in.

It is a cracking trip. The tapirs, the jaguar and the monkeys swinging freely though the trees by their tails are especially popular. We enjoy a picnic-lunch and then it's time to leave for home. 'Everybody in?' 'Yes!' Off we go.

Our friends drop us at home and we go in and make a pot of tea. We call the children and they all come in to the kitchen – except David. We call him again but he doesn't come. One of the other children goes off to his room to get him but he isn't there. Somewhat irritated, I go outside to see if he's playing on the climbing frame, but he isn't. 'Anyone seen David? David! *DAAAAVID!*' Everyone else comes out to join the search. But he doesn't reply. There is no sign of him. Irritation is now giving way to a sort of hollow, knotted feeling in my stomach.

'I bet he went back with the Watsons to their place,' says somebody, hopefully. We ring them up, but he isn't there. They pick up our anxiety and come round in the 'bus. We begin searching the streets around and calling loudly, but there is no sign of him. I try not to think of recent TV reports about the abduction of children – but the anxiety and fear are palpable now.

'Are you sure he came back with us from the zoo?' I ask, trying to keep calm. Yes, everyone is quite sure. They remember it distinctly – who he sat next to, what he said on the way back.

Trying to be helpful and to look on the bright side, one of the children says: 'Well at least the rest of us are here.' Yes they are, and it is true that if you got 90 per cent in your maths exam you would be utterly delighted. But this isn't an exam. This is our son – the son we love with all our hearts. Only 100 per cent will do.

'There's only one thing for it,' I say. 'I'm going back to the zoo.' It is now over an hour since we left the zoo and another 20 minutes to drive back there. I take one of the older children with me and set off at an unsafe speed, taking risks with overtaking, not saying a word, with a very dry mouth, feeling sick.

We turn the final corner and screech to a halt outside the main gate. There, under a tree, is a middle-aged man, gently holding a small child who is beside himself, beyond crying, face covered with tears and snot. It is David. I take him in my arms and we all weep with relief.

We are pathetically grateful. What must this stranger think of us? Leaving our son for nearly an hour and a half at the zoo? I hand David to his sister and he clings to her tightly. We climb back into the car and drive home.

Thank God. He is safe.

The Father said: 'Quick! Bring out the best clothes and put them on him. Put a ring on his finger and shoes on his feet. Kill the prize calf we've been saving and throw a party! Let's rejoice and celebrate! For my son was dead, but now he's alive; he was lost, but now he is found.' And the party began.

From Luke 15

Jesus said: 'the whole point of my coming is to search for and find those who are lost'.

Luke 19.10

Foreigners

When Jesus heard what the Roman Centurion said, he was astonished. 'I have not found faith like this in all Israel,' he said. 'Believe me, crowds will come from East and West to feast with Abraham, Isaac and Jacob in the Kingdom of Heaven. But those who thought they were God's children will be thrown out into the darkness, where there will be weeping and bitter regret.'

From Matthew 8

The infants' assembly does not go too well. I have decided to base it on the Parable of the Good Samaritan, but located in East Barnwell.

'An elderly man gets up early and sets off for the shop for his morning paper. He walks up Whitehill Road, Rawlyn Road and Rayson Way before descending the subway steps to cross Barnwell Road. Unfortunately, hiding in the subway is a gang of naughty boys who knock him over, snatch his wallet and give him a good kicking.'

'Oh,' interrupts a smiling 6-year-old in the second row. 'My dad's in prison for beating up an old man!'

It is not a good start, but I press on, explaining how first a teacher, then the vicar, and finally a policeman all pass by the man without helping, thinking that he's drunk. Then a foreign-language student turns up. She calls for an ambulance on her mobile and stays with him 'til they arrive, even though she is missing her lecture.

Afterwards, I wonder whether I might take a different tack,

if doing that particular parable again. I think the message the kids take home is something like this:

- Don't use the subway – walk across the main road, dodging the traffic.
- If you run out of cash you can always rob somebody.
- If you do get into trouble, don't bother asking the police, teachers or vicars for help – they'll be useless.

Ah well! I begin to reflect on foreign-language students. There are a lot of them in Cambridge. People (including me, at times) complain about them cycling three abreast the wrong way round roundabouts. I've seen it happen. Then I start to think about Stan.

Stan used to worship with us regularly until he fell and broke his hip. It seemed a straightforward operation and he was soon out of hospital. We all expected him to be up and about in a few weeks.

But the weeks turned to months and he still sits in his chair in front of the TV. He doesn't have much in the way of family but I visit him every week, and several other people from church drop in to see how he is. We keep him in our prayers and all encourage him to make an effort, to do the exercises the doctor has shown him and, at least, to have a go at walking into the kitchen. Carers bring him meals, get him up, put him to bed. They are pretty good.

The winter comes and goes. He is taken for a daily course of physiotherapy at the local unit. At first he makes a bit of progress, but before long he is back in the chair. He seems to have lost his confidence, given up. He doesn't appear to trust the frame – or his legs. He just sits and watches TV. As the spring comes round again the number of visitors from the church has dwindled to one, plus me – and I'm now down to a visit every two or three weeks. When we mention him in the prayers on Sunday someone asks me: 'Who's Stan?'

And then he starts to become really frail. In the end he is

re-admitted to hospital with pneumonia and dies almost exactly two years after the fall.

Our pastoral care doesn't seem to have had much stickability.

Except for Zaffi, a Muslim woman from Indonesia who lives three doors down the road. Every day since the accident Zaffi comes in the morning to make him a cup of tea. Every lunch time she pops round to check how he is. Every evening she makes sure he's OK before bed. Every day she asks him if he needs anything from the shops. If she isn't going to be there or can't manage, she gets one of her family to help.

> *'Well,' asked Jesus, 'who was it who proved to be a good neighbour to our Stan?' 'Why the Muslim woman, of course,' came the reply. 'OK,' said Jesus. 'Why can't you go and do the same?'*
>
> See Luke 10

III

Passion

I bind unto myself this day
Christ's death on cross
For my salvation.

From 'St Patrick's Breastplate'

A word of introduction . . .

I serve a hard God.
He walks a stern path
Through the earth.
His voice roars in thunder.
Oceans leap in his wake.
Mountains quake.

He is hard and his way is stone.
Like nails
Driven past bone
And splintered to a tree.

I serve a hard God.
He is stern:
Like love.
And hard:
Like a cross.

Thomas, 1980

Passion means something else these days. It means straining every sinew to make that key tackle which may prove the difference between victory and defeat. It means taking sides, putting yourself on the line, standing up for what you believe, being committed rather than sitting on the fence. It means the single-minded, relentless ambition with which climbers strive for the summit of Everest. It means the wild and urgent necessity of flesh meeting flesh as lovers lose themselves in one another.

Christ's Passion embraces all of his suffering and his death. And 'passion' is not an inappropriate word to use. For Christ is no passive victim to whom bad things happen, as if by chance. He knows, from the very start, that his 'passion' – for freedom, for justice, for the poor, for calling people to a complete turnaround, for throwing out empty gestures in favour of worship which transforms lives, for shaking up the system, for not being afraid to speak or who to say it to – he knows that it will lead, inevitably, to pain, to suffering and to death.

And this suffering is not just about crucifixion. It is about choosing the costly path rather than 'copping out'. It is about facing rejection, betrayal, denial and desertion from your closest friends. It is about being completely on your own. It is about a late-night trial, out of the public gaze, where there is only ever going to be one verdict. It is about being spat on, humiliated, flogged so that the flesh comes off your back in chunks and you can hardly stand up. It is about being nailed to a cross and left to hang, gasping for every breath. It is about being torn apart from the Father and the Spirit from whom you have never parted through all eternity. It is about the despair and pain – not just of the Son, but of the Father and the Spirit, watching in anguish as the only Son dies in agony. It is about the cold, dark tomb and being abandoned, lifeless, in the grave.

Whatever we have been through, are going through, he has been there. The Passion of Christ is everything God suffered, so that by his death, we might have life.

> *We must go everywhere. We must tell people that no pit is so deep that Christ is not deeper still. They will believe us, because we were here.*
>
> Corrie Ten Boom, concentration camp survivor, 1976

Courage

Then Shadrach, Meshach and Abednego said to King Nebuchadnezzar: 'The God who we serve is certainly able to deliver us from the fiery furnace and out of your hands, O King. But if not . . .'

From Daniel 3

I take the No. 2 bus from the top of Sopocachi into the centre of town. It is strange living in La Paz, Bolivia, after Argentina. This is not a Latin culture with a few indigenous people: this is an Aymara Indian culture with some Latin influence. I watch as women with huge, multi-layered skirts, bowler hats, babies slung in the brightly-coloured cloth on their backs and heavy bags of shopping in their hands get on and off the bus.

I stiffen slightly as, at the next stop, a man in an army uniform with a gun under his arm gets on the bus. I have seen the police and army in action in the dark days of the 'desaparecidos' in Argentina. Someone is taken off. The bus moves on. They are never seen again. Everyone else remains silent, too intimidated to talk openly about such things for fear of who may be listening, who may be next. I begin to realize the difference between 'human rights' and 'human privileges'. The latter seem the same until they are suddenly removed without warning. Then there is no court of appeal. No access to lawyers. No visits from family. No one to listen as you cry out from the electric bed. Not even a grave to visit and remember.

As the man gets on, to my utter astonishment, a woman from the back of the bus shouts out: 'Driver, don't let that military pig on our bus!' I brace myself, waiting for the shooting to start. Instead another woman chips in: 'Aren't you ashamed of yourself, working for that scum?' 'Yes,' says another woman, standing up, 'I pity your mother, having a son like you! Get yourself off our bus.' By now half the bus is on its feet. They are beginning to jostle the man. He does not lift his gun. He tries to say that the situation isn't his fault. He's just doing his job. Just obeying orders. But his voice is drowned out by the growing chorus. Within minutes he is manhandled off the bus. The women sit down with broad smiles of satisfaction, smacking their formidable palms. 'That showed him!' We drive on. I look behind. The soldier is dusting himself down as he walks sheepishly towards town.

The Aymara people have suffered greatly over many centuries, conquered in turn by the Incas and the Spanish. They have been fearfully exploited but never broken. Shamefully treated, they remain unbowed. Over the next few months there is a series of marches, demonstrations and strikes. The army respond with tear gas and bullets but the protests continue to gain momentum. 'Campesinos' block all the main roads, bringing the country to a halt. Finally the miners march in from Potosi and Oruru, chewing coca and slinging dynamite around with gay abandon.

Within a year the military government has handed power back to the elected president. A lot of ordinary people suffer in the process. But death is by no means the worst thing that can happen to you. Some things are worth dying for. Like the Desert Fathers, 'they were determined to die *for* something rather than *of* something' (Adam, 2000).

I have, ringing in my ears, the words of Ewan McColl, folk singer and communist. 'Did you alter the face of the city, what change did you make to the world you found?' It takes courage to stand up and be counted. I wonder if I'll have it at the moment of truth?

They were on the road again, walking up to Jerusalem. The disciples were filled with dread and those who followed behind were terrified. Taking the twelve aside Jesus told them plainly what was about to happen: 'Look, we are going to Jerusalem where I will be handed over to the Chief Priests and Scribes, who will condemn me to death and hand me over to the Romans to be killed.'

Mark 10.32, 33

Lord God, give me the courage to make a difference that I ever lived at all.

Remembering

On the night he was betrayed, Jesus took some bread, gave thanks to God, broke it and gave it to the disciples, saying: 'This is my body, given for you. As you do this, remember me. In the same way after supper he took the cup, gave thanks and gave it to them, saying: 'This is the cup of God's New Covenant, sealed with my blood. As you drink it, remember me.'

1 Corinthians 11.23–5

It has been a long day, but only one more appointment to go and then I can put my feet up. I have arranged the funeral visit for 6.30 p.m. That should give me plenty of time to be back for *EastEnders* at 8 p.m. Big night! Will Dirty Dan get his come-uppance?

I knock on the door and Mrs Jackman welcomes me in. 'I'm really sorry to hear about your husband's death,' I say. Tears well up in her eyes. 'Would you like a cup of tea?' she asks. I sit down on the sofa and get out my note-book while she is busy in the kitchen. The tea is served, with custard creams. I dunk a custard cream in the tea and then check the details with her: Mr Trevor Jackman, aged 79, died last Monday, funeral on Thursday at the West Crem, 2 p.m. I blank out part of Wednesday morning as preparation time. Part of the custard cream breaks off and falls to the bottom of the cup. We sort the hymns.

'Who should we include in the prayers?' I ask. 'Well,' she says, 'it's just me really, I suppose.' She goes on to tell me about the major source of sadness in their lives. They were unable to have children. They both loved children, which made it especially difficult to bear. So there is just her, now.

'Of course,' she says, 'we did do a lot of caring for the neighbours' children and for nieces and nephews.' She begins telling me, in great detail, about all the children they have had a hand in bringing up. We are back in the early days just after the war when they first moved in and the roads were not made up. How she would look after Susan and Brian whose dad had been killed in the war while their mum was at work. When Trevor came in from work he'd take off his jacket and get down on the floor to play with them. She emphasizes this again, telling me that a lot of parents don't get down on the floor with their kids, but that she and Trevor always did. And that's important! They'd get out the bag of toys they kept in the cupboard and then they'd all be laughing and playing on the carpet. Then there were the twins – Barry and Tom. What a pair they were! Her cousin's kids. Trevor loved taking them on the common with the kite and down the river with the fishing nets. But you couldn't let them out of your sight for a minute!

She is well into her stride now. I glance at the clock. It is already 7.30 p.m. and we've only got to 1953! I gently try and hurry her but there is no stopping her. The different children, the pain of parting when they move away, the allotment (Trevor's pride and joy), their first car, touring Scotland, the gall bladder op. I have given up all hope of *EastEnders*. And indeed I have forgotten all about Dirty Dan. Now, in my mind, is a vivid picture of Trevor, this straightforward, decent man who worked all his life in the colleges and longed for the children they were never able to have. Despite that sadness, and the terrible pain of Trevor's parting, she is thankful for every one of the 53 years they spent together. As she remembers him, he comes to life. It is as though he is there with us in the room. And, in a way, he is.

As I sit and listen I cannot help thinking of a different story. The one we re-tell, Sunday by Sunday, as we remember the bitter-sweet account of sorrow and pain, thanksgiving and joy, as we break the bread and share the wine which bring to life for us, in a mysterious way we cannot define, the broken body and risen life of Christ, our Saviour. In it, his story becomes our story, and our story finds meaning in his.

At 8.45 I make my way home. I have missed *EastEnders*, but through Mrs Jackman, I have glimpsed something about remembrance, pain and thanksgiving which I will not quickly forget.

Who knows not Love, let him assay
And taste that juice, which on the crosse a pike
Did set again abroach; then let him say
If ever he did taste the like.
Love is that liquor sweet and most divine,
Which my God feels as bloude; but I as wine.

From 'The Agonie' by George Herbert

Night

And God separated the light from the darkness; and the darkness he called night.

Genesis 1.4, 5

There is in God, some say,
A deep and dazzling darkness

From 'The Night' by Henry Vaughan

Why does it always happen at night?

My son has been poorly all day but now, at 10 p.m., he is definitely worse. Should we call out the doctor? Always a difficult choice. They are so busy and what if she comes and says: 'He's OK. What are you worrying about?' We ring up. She arrives about 11 p.m. and measures his peak flow. It is really low. She gives him a cortisone injection and puts him on a Nebulizer. After half an hour he is worse. She calls the hospital and we take him in. We sit anxiously at his bedside while he wheezes for breath inside the oxygen tent. It is now 1.30 a.m., at night.

*

The phone rings. It's the hospice. Could I go down and be with the family, please? Yes, she's just died and they'd like me to come in and say a prayer with them. They are all there, upset, gathered around the bedside. It is just past midnight.

*

'Can you come please – now?' 'Can't it wait 'til the morning?' But I can tell from the cold tone of her voice, which is normally so cheery, that it can't. It's their daughter. She's just been raped, on her way home, at night.

*

The worst thing is that their house has not just been broken into, but deliberately trashed. Furniture and mirrors scratched, drawers emptied out, personal papers torn, stuff smeared across the walls, their most treasured personal mementoes gone. It all happened while they were asleep upstairs, at night.

*

> *Jesus said: 'Have you come out with swords and clubs as if I were a bandit? Day after day I was with you in the temple but you never laid a finger on me. But this is your hour, when the power of darkness rules.'*
>
> Luke 22.52, 53

Betrayed

If it were some enemy taunting me, I could have coped with it.
If it were a rival taking the Mick, I could have just steered clear.
But it was you, my great mate, my bosom buddy, my closest pal.

Psalm 55.12, 13

I listen as Charlie pours out his heart. He could understand it if they'd been rowing or he'd not been bringing in the money. But they haven't and he has. He could even bring himself to forgive her. But his best mate! How could he do this? They've known each other since they were 12, played football in the same team, holidays in Spain, fishing trips, out on the sauce together every Friday night. And all this time it's been going on behind his back. He can see the signs now, of course, looking back. But if you can't trust your best mate – their Best Man! – who can you trust? How could he have been such a fool? And she's taken the kids.

He holds his head in his hands. 'My God! What the hell am I going to do? What the hell am I going to do?' he cries.

It is a familiar story. I have heard it a dozen times before. Betrayed by those you trusted most. Let down by those you loved.

Yes Lord, you know, don't you?

Betrayed

Suddenly a mob approached, with Judas, one of the twelve disciples, leading them. He went up to Jesus as if to embrace him. But Jesus said to him: 'Judas, will you betray the Son of Man with a kiss?' Then all the rest of the disciples cleared off and deserted him.

Luke 22.47, 48; Mark 14.50

Costly Love

Two days before his arrest, while Jesus was eating in Bethany, a woman came in with an alabaster jar of very expensive perfume and poured the whole of it over Jesus and wiped his feet with her hair. The whole house was filled with the power of the fragrance.

But the disciples were appalled. 'That was worth a fortune!' they said. 'What a waste! Why not sell it and give it to the poor?'

But Jesus replied: 'Leave her alone. You will always have the poor with you but you will not always have me. She has done something beautiful, anointing my body for the day of burial. I tell you, wherever the gospel is proclaimed, what she has done will be told in memory of her.'

From Matthew 26 and John 12

The Clinical Theology Association Annual Conference turns out to be one of those bizarre events which contains the best and worst of everything. The main addresses, on 'Supervision', are given by a Canadian Professor and are outstanding. We have 'Bijou Clowning' which, after a slow start, turns out to be hilarious. There are all sorts of side-shows including aromatherapy and all-over body massage (which I am too unliberated to try).

And, of course, there are our 'experiential groups' – a place to share in confidence anything we like, twice a day with eight or nine others. The groups are non-directive. Ours gets off to a slow start, with no one wanting to seem 'pushy' or to make a bid for leadership. No one wants to be the first to admit that they are not quite so together as we are all trying to look.

Then, a woman from Walsall begins to talk about her situation. She tells us that things have not been easy with her husband. He is not been keen on her doing the counselling course and getting so involved in the church. He didn't want her to come on the conference either. It's as though he can't bear her to have a life outside their home. She feels very unsupported. Tomorrow is her wedding anniversary, but she's not looking forward to it, as she's away from home and, in any case, he's bound to forget, as usual. It's like a picture of their marriage, no longer all that important to him. Her openness begins to thaw our defences and, one by one, we start to share things which are more than just superficial.

The following morning the Woman from Walsall comes in beaming from ear to ear. She tells us that a huge bouquet of flowers has arrived from her husband. She is overwhelmed. He has never sent her flowers before and they are very precious to her. She has not even opened them yet. They are standing in a bucket at the side of her bed. She doesn't want to spoil the beautiful wrapping.

We always meet in the same room, with the chairs arranged in a circle by the window. That afternoon we turn up as usual for our group session. Another group has been using the room and has moved the chairs. One of our group arrives early and puts them back, moving them further away from the window, which is a bit draughty. People begin to arrive and we sit down, apart from one man who remains standing outside the group with his arms folded, looking very cross.

'Aren't you going to join us, Brian?' someone asks.

'Who has moved the chairs?' he demands to know.

Janet, who rearranged them, explains that another group had moved them so she put them back in a circle when she arrived.

'They are no longer in the same place as they were before,' he snaps. 'The integrity of the group has been compromised!

We are no longer a group because someone has taken a unilateral decision to change the dynamic without consulting the rest. I can no longer be part of this group – not that there is now a group to be part of.' He is clearly very angry.

'Oh, come off it, Brian,' someone else says. 'That's ridiculous! What does it matter where we sit? It's still the same group of people.'

Somebody else says that they don't feel as strongly as Brian, but they think he's got a point. Janet is really upset. She feels that she has actually done the group a favour by tidying up the mess the other users left and rearranging the chairs. And what thanks does she get? Nothing! She bursts into tears. Someone puts an arm around her. But someone else says that tears are just emotional blackmail on the rest of the group.

The group is rapidly becoming polarized between the mainstream 'pragmatists' and the smaller 'Brian faction'. The nit-picking analysis of the 'chairs event' continues for half an hour. There is a prickly atmosphere and everyone's defences are battened up even tighter than on the day we arrived. The Woman from Walsall quietly gets up and leaves. The bickering continues.

A few minutes later the Woman from Walsall walks back in. She has in her arms the enormous bouquet of flowers. She silently kneels down in the centre of the group and begins to unwrap them. She takes four or five of the best blooms and gives them to Janet, who is still weeping. She kneels down again and takes another handful. The room is quiet now. She walks over and gives them to Brian. He doesn't want to take them but she looks at him and says 'Please, Brian'. He puts out his hands and receives them from her. She goes back to the bouquet and takes some more. One by one she goes around the group, handing each of us in turn the precious flowers. Finally, there is just one left, a red carnation, which she takes for herself, with the card, from the empty wrapping paper. She goes back to her seat and sits down. She is weeping now, and so are we.

Gradually we begin to talk again. Brain talks about how the

chairs being moved had triggered off in him a very painful experience, which he shares with us. Other people, too, begin to plumb the depths and talk about the real stuff of their lives. People listen intently, comment helpfully. When the bell goes for dinner we can't believe the time has run on so quickly. We can't wait until tomorrow's session.

The Woman from Walsall's unexpected, generous, costly love has brought us together, brought us to life.

Love bade me welcome; yet my soul drew back
Guiltie of dust and sinne.
But quick-eyed Love, observing me grow slack,
From my first entrance in,
Drew nearer to me, sweetly questioning,
If I lacked any thing?

A guest, I answered, worthy to be here;
Love said, you shall be he.
I the unkinde, ungratefull? Ah my deare,
I cannot look on thee.
Love took my hand and smiling did reply,
Who made the eyes, but I?

Truth Lord, but I have marr'd them: let my shame
Go where it doth deserve.
And know you not, sayes Love, who bore the blame?
My deare, then I will serve.
You must sit down, says Love, and taste my meat:
So I did sit, and eat.

'Love' by George Herbert

Only One Saviour

Jesus is the one the Bible talks about when it says: 'The stone which the builders rejected has turned out to be the most important of all.'

No one else can save you, for there is no other name in all the world which we can call on to save us.

Acts 4.11, 12

The following day we continue sharing in earnest. Someone says: 'What about you, Alan. You haven't said much.' I am not known for 'not saying much' but we are talking here about deep and difficult stuff, and that does not come so easily.

I begin to tell them about my ministry. As I talk I realize just how burdened I am with the weight of it. I share some of the problems in the parish, some of the conflicts, some of the loads which I am trying to help people bear but which seem too heavy to carry. I tell them about a woman, a few weeks ago, who greeted me at the church door after the service. She was someone with 'insider knowledge' about the most painful issues going on under the surface at church. She grabbed my hand, looked me in the face and said: 'You know, Alan, you've got strength enough for all of us.' I felt flattered and affirmed at the time. But as I thought about it over the next few days, I realized that, actually, I simply didn't have strength to carry all the burdens. In fact, I began to wonder if I could even carry my own, never mind those of all the other people who seemed to be depending on me.

The group listens carefully, sympathizes, makes one or two suggestions. Then we move on to someone else.

At the end of the session we get up to go for coffee. As I am about to leave the Woman from Walsall comes over to me.

'Alan,' she says, 'do you mind if I say something to you?'

'No. Of course not,' I reply, wondering what to expect.

'You know, Alan,' she continues, 'you are not the Saviour. There is a Saviour. And it's not you.' And she turns and goes off for her coffee.

I stand there for a while taking it in. No, I am not the Saviour. It's not all down to me. There is a Saviour. And it's not me. I don't have to bear all the burdens and pain of the world on my shoulders. Someone else, thank God, has done that.

As I walk off to coffee I feel a weight lifting. I look for the Woman from Walsall, but she is already talking to somebody else.

God give us strength.
Strength to hang on.
And strength to let go.

Leunig, 1993

Dying Alone

They went to a place called Gethsemane. He took with him Peter, James and John and began to be stricken with horror and the deepest distress. He said to them: 'My soul is overwhelmed with grief and crushed to the point of death. Stay here and keep watch with me.' Going a little further, he fell to the ground and prayed.

Then he returned to his disciples and found them asleep. 'Simon,' he said, 'are you asleep? Could you not watch with me for even one hour?'

Mark 14.32–5, 37

Beth is a strange woman. She talks endlessly, quite unable to listen, empathize or engage in serious dialogue. 'Monopologue' is, perhaps, the word. Or maybe 'narcissistic'. Despite all her talking over several visits I feel I do not know her at all. Not surprisingly she is completely alone. No family, no visitors, no friends at all.

But now she is unable to speak. The brain tumour has made her speech completely unintelligible. Finally, she has given up trying.

As I stand by her bed in the hospice I take her limp, clammy hand and look into her eyes. What she cannot express in words is all there in her eyes. They are full of foreboding, of anguish, of fear. This is not a woman at peace. This is a woman terrified of imminent death.

I say a few platitudes, recite a Psalm. And then there is nothing else to say. She has not blinked or taken her eyes off me. They are not comforted by my words or my presence. I hear the words of Jesus ringing in my ears: 'Could you not watch with me for one hour?' I feel the beads of sweat on my forehead. I glance at the clock on the wall. I have been here seven minutes.

After ten minutes I say a prayer, bid farewell and leave. I slump into the car, completely exhausted.

I am sorry, Beth. I am sorry, Lord.

I could not watch with you. I could not watch even half an hour.

You will have to go to your death, alone.

The Silence of the Lambs

Herod interrogated him at some length, but Jesus made no answer. Pilate said to him: 'Can't you see how many charges they're bringing against you? Why don't you defend yourself?' But Jesus made no further reply

From Luke 23 and Mark 15

I wish I wasn't so defensive! Somebody asks if it was me that spilled the paint. Instead of simply saying 'Yes; sorry', I go into a long explanation about how, actually, it wasn't my fault, because someone else had left it in a stupid place and, in any case, I'm not the only one to have spilled paint in this house. After the preliminaries I am now in full flow, taking the high ground. 'Look,' I say, pointing, '*these* paint marks have been here for at least six months! Now that *definitely* wasn't me!' QED.

Carboncito

I arrive earlier than usual in the truck and, as I approach the village, wave to Don Pintado. He is a 'Chaqueno', a Spanish-speaking rancher, who also happens to be the local butcher. He rides his horse slowly along, leading a scrawny-looking bullock by a rope. Two of his sons ride in behind him. I feel sorry for Don Pintado's horse. Don Pintado's diet consists of a kilo of barbequed meat for lunch, another kilo for supper, red wine, bread and a sort of herb tea. Oh! And a cold meat selection for breakfast. It's no wonder he is grossly overweight and has liver problems.

'Come and join us for the barbeque,' he calls. I thank him. Actually, I am early so, after calling at the carpentry workshop, I go along to the tree where he has tethered the bullock. Already there is a fire going, with the metal grill on top. There is no butcher's slab. The animal's skin will serve as a table as the carcass is dissected. Soon the meat will be hanging from the tree and the prize portion pulsating on the fire for Don Pintado and guests.

His sons tie the animal's legs together and push it onto its side. They grab the horns and pull back the head to expose its neck. A crowd has gathered. There is a group of smiling women at the front holding empty 'Nido' milk tins.

Don Pintado steps forward. He unsheathes the knife. With a swift skilful slice he makes a six-inch superficial cut through the skin along the throat. Then, in an instant, he plunges in the knife. I wince. Blood shoots forth like a hose-pipe. The women dash forward, holding the cans in turn to catch the dark red stream. Black pudding tonight!

The worst bit for me is the fearful, harrowing, low, moaning death-cry, which goes on for what seems an eternity until, at last, the flow abates, the moaning stops and the animal falls limp.

Pigs are even worse. You can hear their squealing and screeching two or three hundred yards away as they bleed to death.

But sheep and lambs don't make a sound.

Cruelly oppressed and afflicted, he did not open his mouth.
Like a lamb at the slaughter-house,
Like a sheep, that before its shearers is silent,
He never said a word.

From Isaiah 53

Forgiveness

'Father, forgive them, for they have no idea what they are doing.'

Luke 23.34

People say to me: 'Why did Jesus have to die on the cross? Why couldn't God just forgive us?' But forgiveness is costly. It doesn't come cheap.

The youth group is walking the Taquesi Trail. These are kids from poor families who do not have the resources to equip themselves properly for such a trip, which involves a three-day walk across a high mountain pass, part of it above the snow-line. I express my concern about the wisdom of the venture, but am told that the kids are determined to go. At the eleventh hour they are still short of the basics. 'You've got a tent, haven't you? Could we borrow it?' they ask.

I feel 'Tangoed.' 'You do know how to put it up, don't you? It was a wedding present, so you will look after it carefully won't you?' They give firm reassurances but I feel apprehensive as I hand it over.

Several days after they return I ask about the tent. 'Oh, don't worry. Jorge's got it. He'll bring it back tomorrow.' After several more enquiries that make me look like a killjoy-ogre, the tent is finally returned. I thank them warmly.

It feels a bit damp from the outside so the following day I decide to pitch it in the garden to dry it out. As I unpack it my heart sinks. It is thick with mud, there is a hole in the waterproof groundsheet, half of the pegs are missing, as well as several stays and, worst of all, there are two tears in the flysheet fabric.

I speak angrily to one of the leaders, who disclaims all responsibility. He says more young people turned up than expected so they didn't have enough tents. It was very cold and they had to split the main tent from the groundsheet and wrap themselves in both to try and keep warm and dry. 'Did you expect me to let them freeze to death?' he asks incredulously.

It takes me quite a while to swallow my annoyance and forgive them. And it comes at a price. It costs me £120 for a new tent!

*

Aunty Betty lives with her son, Michael, in a small prefab. Life is not easy. Her husband, Denis, left her when Michael was a baby. He has not been in touch and has never paid a penny of the maintenance he owes. She works hard at the local nursery to make ends meet and doesn't complain. And she will not hear a word against Denis.

Eighteen years later a letter arrives in the post. As she shares it with the family they are incensed. 'The damn nerve of the man!' says Uncle Mick. 'I'll kill the bastard!' It is a letter from Denis. He has been living with another woman since he left Betty. He has had two sons by her who are now 15 and 17. The 'other woman' has recently died of cancer, he tells her, and they are really struggling. Of course he now realizes what a fool he's been and how it's really Betty he loved all the time. Can she come down to Bristol and live with him again, please? Oh, and look after him and the boys?

The family's anger gives way to incredulity as Betty explains that she is still legally married to him and that she loves him. She has never, for her part, broken her marriage vows and she doesn't intend to start now. Despite the pleading of her sisters and her mother's tears, she plans to move down to Bristol the following week.

And go she does. It is painful and difficult. Denis's boys thought he was married to *their* mother, not Betty. They refuse to believe that Michael is really Denis's son. Relationships are strained. But she is determined. She sticks with him, brings up the two boys as well as her own son, loves him through all his hair-brained schemes and unrealistic ambitions and finally, 25 years later, she nurses him through cancer and sits at his bedside as he breathes his last.

I think about this astonishing woman, who was my godmother. What did it cost *her* to forgive, day after day, week after week, year after year? Not saying, time and again: 'Well, that's just like you. That's exactly what you did the last time.'

The price is beyond my comprehension.

*

I listen to the news. It has been another day of bloodshed in the Middle East. A suicide bomber has killed 20 Israeli teenagers in a disco and, in retaliation, Israeli tanks have blasted Palestinian positions, killing several soldiers and a number of women and children. We await the report of the Mitchell Commission with little optimism. What can he say? 'We have totalled it up and it would appear that there have been 247 more Palestinians killed than Israelis. Allowing for statistical error, we reckon that if we kill 230 Israelis, that will be about quits and we can all shake hands and start again from scratch.' Somehow, I don't think so.

Then an astonishing piece of news. A young Palestinian pharmacist called Mazen Julani has been shot dead by an Israeli settler. His father, Lufti, despite his grief and anger, decides to donate Mazen's organs for transplant. Four people benefit from the transplanted organs. The major beneficiary receives a life-saving heart transplant. What is astonishing is that they are all Jews.

*

Judgement can no longer keep track of centuries of wrongs. There is no end to the cycle of hatred and reprisal. Only mercy and forgiveness offer a way out. Forgiveness which, instead of returning hurt for hurt, takes the pain, bears it, does not hit back, but returns good instead.

But who is up to this kind of forgiveness? I think of Aunty Betty, Lufti Juliani, Nelson Mandela, one or two people from Northern Ireland. There are not many who can bear the pain and pay this high a price.

Surely he has taken upon himself our suffering
And born all our sorrows.
We thought he was being punished by God for his own sins,
But in fact he was wounded for our wrongdoing,
Crushed with pain for our faults.
The punishment that fell on him has brought us peace
And the blows he suffered have made us whole.

From Isaiah 53

I think of how I feel when my own children suffer. How often do people say to me: 'If only it could be me instead of him?'

Yet each of us is a child of God. So every child who is bullied, every person beaten up, every woman raped or abused at home, every persecuted minority, every black slave, every one tortured for their religious belief, every African to have a leg blown off by a landmine, every mother who will never receive her son back from war, every Asian to die of malnutrition through the greed of others, every victim of torture, every single one, throughout history, is a dearly loved child of God. I try and imagine the cumulative weight of all the appalling deeds of humanity since time began. I simply cannot. And yet all this pain, this grief, this anguish falls upon Christ at the cross. He bears it all, without striking back in retaliation, and says instead: 'Father, forgive them.'

And this is not just the suffering of the Son, while the Father sits in heaven, looking on with satisfaction that the price has finally been paid. No! This is the pain of the Father, seeing his only Son in anguish, dying in humiliation. This is the agony of the Holy Spirit, torn from the Son with whom she has been in perfect harmony from all eternity. The cross is the whole of the Trinity crying out in pain and agony, ripped apart by our rebellion, torn asunder by the appalling evil done on the face of the earth since time immemorial. The cross is the place where Father, Son and Holy Spirit, together, bear the appalling price of our salvation, the incalculable cost of our forgiveness.

Alas! No man or woman can ever redeem themselves,
No one can pay to God the price of their life,
For the cost of a human life is too great.
It is beyond our power to pay a ransom that would cheat the grave
And let us live for ever.

Psalm 49.7, 8

Unforgiven

'Forgive us our sins, as we forgive those who have done us wrong. For if you forgive others their failures, your Father in heaven will also forgive you yours. But if you do not forgive others, you will not be forgiven either.'

Matthew 6.12–15

We always knew it would not be easy helping the two communities to move and settle together on a single plot of land. There was a great deal of consultation and everyone agreed it was the only possible way forward. The land on which they had been living for centuries was actually 'fiscal' land, government owned. And the government had made it quite clear they weren't planning to give it to the indigenous people. Worse, much of it had already been sold for large-scale 'Agribusiness' and the trees were being felled at an alarming rate.

The precise details of how things will work out are negotiated by the community leaders. A major issue is the village co-operative shop. Who will run it? Can we trust someone from the *other* community with *our* money and *our* supplies?

Soon the well is dug, roads are cut, the farm area is cleared and fenced. School, clinic, carpentry workshop and church are all built. And, of course, the shop. Two people are appointed, Jorge and Ernesto, one from each community, to run it. They are both pillars of the church and considered, in their respective communities, to be above reproach.

People start arriving in lorry-loads. Over the weeks they begin to settle in. Houses are built, the school starts to function, the first crops are planted. There is a great spirit of hopefulness and optimism. It reminds me of the Exodus.

But there are rumblings. The people from the San Pedro community begin to suspect that those from Salinas are getting a better deal than they are in the shop. Unsurprisingly, those from Salinas think the same thing, in reverse.

The grumblings gradually get worse. Tension mounts. (I am reminded of the Exodus again!) Jorge says that, when he is not looking, Ernesto is taking money from the till. Ernesto denies it and accuses Jorge of stealing flour and sugar. They are no longer on speaking terms. One day it comes to a head when they refuse to work with each other and the store is closed. It's the only store for miles, so this is serious.

The community leaders decide to tackle the issue head-on. There is an open-air meeting in which Jorge and Ernesto are asked in turn to express their grievances. Most of the village turn up to hear. As they each accuse the other, things begin to turn ugly. People are pushing and shouting. I fear a mass brawl may break out.

Then a woman speaks. She asks Jorge and Ernesto if they have any concrete evidence of wrongdoing. Neither has. She reminds them of why they moved here, of their hopes and aspirations. She reminds them of the communities they've left where the land was being cleared and fenced and where they could no longer make a living. She reminds them that there is work here for everyone and that no one is hungry. She reminds them of their children and grandchildren who will grow up with decent health care, with an education and with hope for the future. Finally she points them to the main building in the centre of the village – the church – and to the cross on its roof. 'Don't you remember that Christ died so that you could be forgiven?' she says. 'Is it too much for you to forgive one another given all that Christ suffered to forgive you?'

There is silence. Jorge and Ernesto look at their feet. After several minutes Ernesto looks at Jorge. 'I'm sorry,' he says. 'I am sorry too,' says Jorge. They shake hands and embrace. There is a time of prayer for forgiveness all round. And then applause. This is a stoic people, not given much to celebration. But now there is laughter and rejoicing. The store opens for the afternoon shift.

*

Six months later I drive into the village. People are milling around the centre. It is 10 a.m. but the store is closed. 'What's happened?' I ask. 'Is somebody sick?' 'No. It's Jorge. He walked out of the store last night and says he won't come back. Ernesto can't run it on his own.'

I walk round to Jorge's house. He is sitting outside by the open fire. He does not look up to greet me. I sit down beside him. After a while I enquire: 'What's gone wrong?'

'I knew it would never work,' he says. 'Ernesto has been at it again. Hand in the till. Taking sugar and flour home when I'm not looking. Fiddling the books. Accusing me.'

'Do you have any evidence?'

'Ah! He's too sly. You can never catch him red-handed. But I know it's going on. I've recorded all the times I've noticed something go missing or when he's deliberately insulted me.'

He takes a battered old piece of paper from his inside pocket and carefully unfolds it. 'Look,' he says.

In the centre of the paper is a picture of a man. 'That's me,' he says. Around it are arrows pointed inwards, looking like sharp, poison darts. There are about 40 of them. Each one has a date written on it and the name 'Ernesto'. He begins to explain to me what each one means.

'On this occasion,' he complains, 'I went out for a minute and when I came back the flour sack had gone down by about a third – and there were no customers. This one was when I was on my way to the clinic and he deliberately snubbed me. This one here is when I saw him laughing at me with some of the men from his village. This is when there was a 5,000-peso note missing from the till.'

As he continues to speak I look at the dates. These dates do not go back six months. They go back 14 years! – well before the new village came into being, or was even thought of; long before the time, six months ago, when, so I thought, all had been forgiven.

I talk to him about the pain he feels. Then I ask him why he has held on to it all these years. Why didn't he destroy the paper six months ago when there was the opportunity for a new start? Why doesn't he think again about the cross and all it means? Why can't he forgive Ernesto and begin again? Why not throw the list on the fire, right now, and burn it?

'No,' he says as he sits erect. 'He has gone too far. The wounds are deep and will not heal. There are too many scars. He has done me great harm for too long. I cannot forgive him.'

We sit in silence for some time. Then he carefully folds up the piece of paper and puts it back in his inside pocket. I bid him farewell and leave, heavy hearted.

> *Some say the world will end in fire,*
> *Some say in ice.*
> *From what I've tasted of desire*
> *I hold with those who favor fire.*
> *But if it had to perish twice,*
> *I think I've known enough of hate*
> *To say that for destruction ice*
> *Is also great*
> *And would suffice.*
>
> Frost, 1973

Free Gift

'There's no such thing as a free lunch.'

Popular saying

'It was God's grace which saved you. It's not your own doing – it's God's free gift.'

Ephesians 2.8

It is Saturday morning. We are having a lie-in when the phone goes.

'Oh hello Grandma, how are you?'

'Something terrible's happened,' she says, sounding very upset.

'Oh no. Is it my Dad?'

'No. Not that. But it's terrible. Jack and Nora have given us a car!'

They have known Jack and Nora since before the war. They used to go dancing together at Mark Haltman's Ballroom in Leeds and have stayed friends ever since. Jack and Nora are a bit older than Mum and Dad and are now rather frail and almost housebound. Each week Mum and Dad get into their clapped-out old Fiat and drive across Leeds to visit them. Mum bakes a cake, some buns or takes a plant. She chats to Nora while Dad takes Jack to Morrison's for the weekly shop. It's a good half-day trip.

Nora and Jack have been very grateful indeed for their friendship and help. It's one thing to lend a hand occasionally, but week in, week out, year in, year out – that's something else.

They think about leaving Mum and Dad some money in the will, but that might cause problems in their family. In any case, what Mum and Dad really need is to replace the old Fiat, which is more rust than paint. And the sooner the better. Yes! That's what they'll do – the perfect surprise.

So one Saturday morning in November at 8.30 a.m. the bell rings and Mum goes down in her nightgown to see who it is.

'Special delivery for Mr and Mrs Hargrave,' he says: 'sign here.'

She signs, expecting him to hand over a parcel, but he doesn't.

'What is it love?' she asks.

'It's a new car,' he replies, very matter-of-fact. 'I've parked it in the drive.'

She looks out. There it is, in the drive, a brand-new Ford Fiesta. As she stares in disbelief she notices the next-door neighbour looking through the curtain.

'Oh no love,' she says. 'I think you've made a mistake. We haven't ordered a car.'

'No mistake,' he insists. 'It's a present from Mr and Mrs Jack Mason, with their love.' He shows her the card. She shouts for Ronnie. He comes down in his pyjamas. She explains what's happened. Despite their pleading, the man refuses to take it away. That's when she rings us.

'Well,' we exclaim. 'That's wonderful, Mum! They are obviously really grateful for all your love for them, and they've wanted to express their love for you. What a tremendous gift.'

'No!' she says, her voice trembling but firm. 'You don't understand. I mean, it's not for the likes of us – we've never had a new car in our lives. We can't afford it. We've done nothing to deserve this. In any case, we don't want to be beholden. And the neighbours are buzzing! We just can't accept it. What are we going to do?'

As she speaks I think of how God's free gift of grace is so difficult to accept in a society where we firmly believe that everything must be worked for and that, as with anything else, there must be a catch.

- 'It's not for the likes of us.' Wrong. It *is* for us – for absolutely every last one of us.
- 'We can't afford it.' No we can't. We can never afford the price of grace. But we don't need to. Christ has paid the price on the cross.
- 'We've done nothing to deserve this.' Right. We haven't. But this is a gift, not payment for services rendered.
- 'We don't want to be beholden.' But maybe it really isn't like that. This isn't about being obliged or needing to repay. It is about being loved and responding to the one who loves us.

We talk on the phone for a long time. They are both in tears. They visit Jack and Nora (in the old Fiat!) and have several 'four-hanky sessions' with them. Meanwhile, the blue Fiesta sits in the drive, untouched. But eventually, after about a month, they accept it. They get in and drive it away.

Jack and Nora died some time after. But Mum and Dad, with thankful hearts, enjoyed their free gift for the rest of their lives.

Let everyone who is thirsty come
And let anyone who wishes come
Come and take the water of life
As a free gift, without price.

Revelation 22.17

In the End, Love

Having loved his disciples from the start, Jesus loved them to the very end.

John 13.1

I drive around for a good 20 minutes before I eventually find a space, at the wrong end of the hospital. I walk along the seemingly endless corridors but, as I turn a corner, something catches my eye.

Ahead of me, moving painfully slowly, is a wheelchair. In it an elderly woman is slumped to one side. She seems to be asleep. She is very drawn and thin, and has that fearful yellow complexion that makes you think the worst.

Pushing the wheelchair is a wizened old man who does not look in much better shape than she does. He shuffles along, steadying himself on the handles. He is talking to her.

'Don't worry love,' he reassures her, 'we'll have you home before you know it.'

Her eyes open a fraction. 'You'll have to *put* me in a home, more like,' she replies, weakly.

He leans forward with his face close to hers. 'Not while I've got breath,' he affirms, with all the strength and tenderness he can muster.

I am past them now. As I get to the corner, I glance back. He continues to shuffle along, pushing the load which he cannot manage but will not lay down. I wonder which of them will go first. One thing for sure. He will love her to the end.

Their final blazon, and to prove
Our almost-instinct almost true:
What will survive of us, is love.

Larkin, 1990

IV

Resurrection

Christ's bursting from the spiced tomb
His riding up the heavenly way
His coming at the day of doom
I bind unto myself today.

From 'St Patrick's Breastplate'

A word of introduction . . .

Alleluia! Christ is Risen.
He is risen indeed. Alleluia!
Easter Liturgy

Resurrection shouts from the rooftops that death is not the end. It tells us that, when all seems lost, love triumphs over hatred, good overcomes evil, life conquers death. Death is swallowed up in victory. One day, as sure as the dawn follows the night, there will be an end to weeping, pain and grief. One day there will be freedom, justice, and, at last, peace for evermore. But for now, we live between Passion and Resurrection, between life and death.

Perhaps that's why, for me, resurrection is the hardest thing to talk about. It never seems to stand alone. In my own experience, resurrection has almost always been linked to moments of 'passion'. Indeed, without death there is no resurrection. Yet as I read John's Gospel, in particular, Christ's 'glorification' seems deliberately to mean both his death on the cross and his rising in glory. And so often in my experience, resurrection is not about change in circumstances, but about changes inside me.

The American Old Testament scholar Walter Brueggemann, in his excellent book *The Message of the Psalms* (1984) (you only need to read the Introduction to get the message), suggests that there are three basic types of psalm which describe our ongoing experience of life.

First there are psalms of orientation such as Psalm 1. Here is the solid bedrock of faith on which we stand – like the tree planted by water which stands firm and yields its fruit in season. We feel that we can never be shaken.

But then there are psalms of disorientation. Tragedy strikes. It is as though the rug has been pulled from under our feet. We can find no solid ground on which to stand. The old certainties do not seem to help. We are floundering, sinking.

> *We could understand it if we'd forgotten you, O God, but we haven't. We've followed you faithfully and now look – disaster, disgrace, defeat, death. Wake up God! What are you messing at. Get up and help us, please!'*
>
> From Psalm 44

Thesc, says Brueggemann, are songs of disarray, of lament. (And it is a tragedy that in the church we seem to have lost the music of lament in our worship.) They are, in New Testament terms, psalms of the cross.

> *'My God, my God, why have you abandoned me?'*
>
> Psalm 22 and Mark 15.34

But finally there are psalms of new orientation.

> *'Oh, sing to the Lord a new song,' says the psalmist.*
>
> (e.g. Psalm 96)

Surprising, unexpected, when hope is gone and all is despair and darkness, we receive the touch of God's grace. And suddenly, though nothing has changed, everything has changed. It is transformation. It is glory. It is resurrection.

Of course, any given Psalm may speak to us at one time of the pain of the cross, and at another of hope renewed. The same is true of these stories. Many of them could have been included in two or more different sections of this book. And the same will be true of your own stories, as you reflect on them again and again over time. This should not surprise us. For it is the work of the Holy Spirit to meet us, unexpectedly, just where we are, in life, in death, in resurrection.

> *Love is born*
> *With a dark and troubled face.*
> *When hope is dead*
> *And in the most unlikely place*
> *Love is born*
>
> Leunig, 1993

By Name

The Lord, who created you, says this:
'Do not be afraid, for I have saved you.
I have called you by name.
You are mine.'

Isaiah 43.1

The doctor tells us he doesn't think the baby will arrive for at least another month. Bit of a problem. We decide that Annie will stay in the provincial capital but that I'll have to go back up north, to the 'sticks', where we work. 'That sounds sensible,' says the doctor. 'Have you decided what you are going to call the baby?' 'No, not yet.' We've always thought names were important, but two recent discoveries have served to emphasize this even more.

First of all, we find that we cannot just give our new baby any name we choose. No! There is an approved government list. Zak, Megan and Harriet are not on it. Not that we wanted any of those, but they suddenly seem more attractive for being forbidden.

The second discovery is more salutary. Until relatively recently the indigenous communities of the Argentine Chaco were essentially 'non-people'. They had no documents and therefore no rights as citizens. When the amnesty finally came, which allowed them to register and get an identity document, there was initially great rejoicing. Unfortunately, some of the officials, with little regard for those they considered illiterate savages, took the opportunity to play a joke or two. Especially with the many who couldn't read.

'Name?' they demand of the next man in the queue. 'Jose Gonzalez' comes the quiet reply. 'Pescado Oloroso' types the official on the identity document. Next. Name? 'Modesto Prado.' 'Right,' says the official, smirking at his colleague, 'Modesto Prado it is.' But he types 'Pies Podridos' on the identity card. And so it is that, for the rest of their lives, Jose Gonzalez and Modesto Prado have to live with the indignity, at every checkpoint, on every official document, in every government office, of being called 'Smelly Fish' and 'Rotten Feet'.

It is no wonder that their true names, their tribal names, they never reveal to a living soul outside their closest family.

I have only been back up north for a day when the message comes through on the twice-a-day radio communication. My wife is in labour. She went into the clinic at 7 a.m. My boss already has the truck revved up and ready to go. But it's a four-hour drive and it's already 9 a.m. I know in my heart I'm not going to make it.

And, sure enough, I don't. The baby is born at 10 a.m. I arrive at 2 p.m. Mother and baby are doing well but have been put in a ward with one other woman, who has TB. We decide that an immediate departure for 'home' is required. Our 3-year-old has been looked after by friends round the corner. She comes running in, beaming from ear to ear. 'Can I hold her?' she asks. We sit her on a sofa, in the corner. The Mothercare sandals on the end of her legs do not quite reach the edge of the cushion. Annie carefully lays the tiny bundle on her lap. She gently enfolds it in her arms.

'What are we going to call her?' she asks, excitedly.

'Her name is Laura Jane,' comes the reply.

'Laura Jane,' she repeats. 'Laura Jane! We're all very pleased. We're all very pleased!'

When I register the birth the following day I watch carefully as the official types the name. There will be no 'mistake' this time. She is very clearly ours.

At some time in the next few years Jose Gonzalez will lie on his bed in his hut, knowing he is about to die. He will call his children to his side and speak to them in his own name – not 'Smelly Fish' nor even 'Jose Gonzalez' but the secret tribal name he was given at birth, the name only they will know. He will address them by their own names, the special secret ones he himself gave them when they were born. And, as he dies, they will know that they are loved and blessed and that, without a shadow of a doubt, they are his.

Like Mary, who, on that first Easter morning, does not recognize her Lord until he calls her, by name. Then she knows who he is. Then she knows he is alive. Then she knows who she is.

Mary stands at the tomb weeping. She sees Jesus, but doesn't recognize him. 'Woman,' he says to her 'why are you weeping? Who are you looking for?'

Thinking it is the gardener she replies: 'Look, sir, if you've taken his body, please just tell me where you've put him and I'll go and get him.'

Jesus says to her: 'Mary.'

Mary turns, throws her arms round him and exclaims: 'Master! It's you!'

From John 20

Foot and Mouth

In its way there can hardly be anything in the world to beat the Vale of Clwyd.

Gerard Manley Hopkins

I arrive at the retreat centre on a fine morning in late May. The spring blossom abounds in the hedgerows. From the house I can clearly see the square tower of St Asaph Cathedral across the valley and the 'Marble Church' spire beyond. To my right the river gently bends its way towards the coast, which disappears by Great Orme's Head. From there the hills sweep away to the south. In the distance I can make out the characteristic shape of Tryfan, with the Glyders and Snowdon to the left. I don't have the car with me, so walking will be restricted to the local hills. Nevertheless, I can hardly wait.

But the first path off the narrow road has a large notice with red lettering.

'Foot and Mouth Disease. Path closed.' And all the others say the same.

With my mind, of course, I understand it, but, as the days pass, road-walking begins to grate and I spend more time indoors, longing for the freedom of the hills. A few days of feeling sorry for myself lead to more serious thoughts. I think of our recent trip to Uganda. The day after we arrive, a Wednesday as I recall, we wander up the hill to the cathedral. We are unable to go in because there is some sort of service going on. After some time, people in their Sunday best, well over a hundred of them, begin to file out. Curiosity gets the better of me and I approach a woman, asking, 'Excuse me, is it a wedding or something?' 'Oh no!' she exclaims. 'We are having a special service of prayer for farmers in Britain with foot and mouth disease.' I am stunned. I feel ashamed. If we called people in Cambridge to pray together for the AIDS crisis in Uganda, I wonder how many would turn up?

On the Welsh roads I have passed several farms with buckets filled and straw mats soaked with antiseptic. I begin to imagine the farmers, day after day, week after week, month after month, cooped up on the farm, unable to leave, unable to socialize, unable to load up the sheep for market or even for a different pasture. I think of them sitting at night, anxious, restless, waiting in fear for the knock on the door that says 'Mr Thomas? I'm very sorry to have to tell you but there's been an outbreak next door. We'll be coming tomorrow morning. Yes, I'm afraid so. It will mean all of them. Yes, the lambs too.'

I think of the disciples in the Upper Room on that fearful Saturday. Their leader is dead. The religious authorities have successfully got rid of him. Smart move, just before the festival. People will have too many other things on their minds to kick up much of a fuss. Now for the clean-up operation. Shouldn't take too long. A dozen or so ringleaders – that should stop it spreading! The rest won't cause us too much bother. Meanwhile, the disciples sit, terrified, waiting for the knock of death.

It is the seventh day of my retreat when my 'director' says 'Oh, by the way, did you know that the Council has re-opened some of the paths? Not all of them, but the Offa's Dyke trail is open, just up here on the hill.'

I go back to my room, grab my day-sack, map, water bottle, walking stick, and set off up the narrow road. I stride out up the steep road to where it branches left. The path goes to the right. There is a new notice with a large green tick on the top. There are still precautions to be taken, it says, but the path is open!

I climb the stile and set off up the wooded track. I'll just walk for half an hour and then head back. My heart sings as I stride out under the green canopy of the arching beeches with their fresh green coats. I really ought to be thinking about turning back. No, just a bit further. I am going ridiculously fast. Must slow down; must stop for a rest. But the legs keep on and up at the same cracking pace, moving from memory of younger and slimmer days. I can feel my heart pounding and think of my wife's wise words: 'Don't forget to stop and take regular drinks of water. Don't get dehydrated.' The bottle is in the rucksack. Stopping to get it is impossible. I steam on, lathered in sweat. If I carry on I will miss the Eucharist – or worse, lunch! I am on the open moor now, yet still I cannot stop, not yet.

I walk in a wide horseshoe and come, at last to a place where a rough cross, made of railway sleepers, marks the top of the ridge, surrounded by yellow gorse. I slump down with my back against the cross, panting for breath, enjoying the fabulous views of the valley, the sea and Snowdonia beyond. I take the bottle out of my rucksack and drain it all in one go. I feel the wind in my face, its strength ripping at my coat. I feel the freedom, like life after death. My heart soars within me.

There will be other dark days and more 'knocks of death' to come.

But for now, the paths are open! Alleluia!

He is Risen! Alleluia!

Rain

On the last and greatest day of the feast Jesus called out in a loud voice: 'If anyone is thirsty, let them come to me and drink. Anyone who believes in me can drink their fill. As the Bible says: "Rivers of living water shall flow from your heart."' He said this about the Holy Spirit, who all those who believed were going to receive.

John 7.37–9

Rukungiri Town, Uganda

It is another hot day. Clouds blow over the hills to the south. But here the sun is shining brightly. Adrine peels the Matooke and looks glum. We need the rain, she says, as she has done every day since we arrived. The beans, maize, tomatoes, bananas are all wilting. The boys are having to wander further and further afield to find grass for their cows. The water storage tanks have been empty for a while. A steady stream of neighbours arrives to fill their jerry cans from the capped spring at the end of the garden. The town pump has broken again and people are queuing for water wherever they can find it.

'It looks as though it might rain today,' I comment, hopefully. She shakes her head. 'I don't think so,' she replies. 'The wind is in the wrong direction.'

That afternoon I walk up to meet Eric at his office. The path is dry and dusty and the thin stream across the track, just before it turns up hill towards the cathedral, is hardly a trickle now.

It is at 5.30 p.m., when we are about to set off home, that the rain begins. It is steady, light rain. Not quite what we need but welcome all the same. 'We'll wait for it to abate and then go,' says Eric. After a few minutes it eases to a drizzle and we set off. I have a cagoul which we put over our shoulders as we walk back along the damp path. At least it has laid the dust. Then the rain starts to pick up again. We carry on. Nearly halfway home now, so not to worry.

By that well-known law, we are almost exactly halfway home (too far to go back, committed to going on) when the heavens open. The rain pours down in sheets. We arrive at the thin stream, which has now become a torrent. Jumping over it in tandem, while holding a single cagoul between us, is not easy and we don't quite make the far shore. We continue to hold the cagoul above us as we walk single file up the track, which has itself become a stream now. It has ceased to serve any useful purpose as we are both soaked, but we are too polite to suggest this, lest the other still feels he is deriving some benefit.

We arrive home and rush for the cover of the overhanging roof. It is still warm, so no point rushing in to get changed. We simply sit and watch. The rain bounces off the tin roof like machine-gun fire. The swollen gutters are pouring water into the large concrete catchment tanks. The first is almost full and the second will soon be on its way. A damp chicken wanders miserably around the concrete patio, which is now a sheet of water, flowing over the steps and onto the beans and bananas below. Children are playing and laughing in the mud outside.

Adrine is in the cook-house, checking the sweet potatoes in the oven. She laughs and grins broadly as she shouts across the patio above the noise of the storm.

'I think we'll be OK now,' she says.

Come Holy Ghost and pour down upon us.
Refresh us with the sweet rain of your Spirit.

Renewal

I pray incessantly for the conversion of the prodigal son's brother. Ever in my ears rings the dread warning: 'The one has awoken from his life of sin. When will the other awaken from his life of virtue?'

Camara, 1981

It has been a bad week. The church, which meets in our living-room, has been growing steadily over the past two years. But now, a crisis. I remember the words of my previous boss. 'Never sell your car to a friend – it'll end in tears.' Unfortunately, this is exactly what has happened. One of our leading church members has sold their car to another church member. The car turns out to be a dud. The recipient, not wanting to cause trouble, 'shares this for prayer' with everyone else in the church, while failing to talk to the people who sold it to them. They only get wind of it second-hand and are annoyed, because they believe they sold it in good working order, below the market value.

Relationships have become seriously strained and I try and intervene to 'help' matters. The curate at our church in Birmingham, years ago, had a great maxim. 'If you put your foot in it, don't wiggle it about.' I have wiggled it about and now things are even worse than before.

In the middle of all this a Bolivian friend, pastor of one of the free churches, rings me up. 'Hi Alan. We've got a guy coming to do some leadership training next weekend. What I hadn't realized is that he doesn't speak any Spanish. Could you translate some of the sessions for us?'

'What is he like?' I ask.

'Well, from what I can gather he has a tremendous ministry in renewal of burnt-out church leaders.'

I am a burnt-out church leader so it sounds right up my street, though I don't mention that to Julio. 'OK,' I reply and we fix up the timetable.

But when I meet Clancy O'Rourke my heart sinks. His first message majors on the need for repentance. What he seems to mean by that is that we should all turn away from left-wing activity and vote in a good, clean, born-again president like Ronald Reagan. Then the whole country will be blessed, just like they are in the USA. There doesn't seem to be much difference in Clancy's mind between being a Christian and being a Republican. I think of all the damage US foreign policy has done to Bolivia over the years. The stockpiling of tin to lower tin prices which has destroyed the mining industry. The heavy-handed attitude to 'coca' growers which means destroying a centuries-old way of life.

I think of the Aymara legend that relates how one of the gods, seeing the great exploitation of the indigenous people by the Spanish 'Conquistadores' gave the people the coca plant, to help them cope with the difficult conditions of life on the altiplano and the harsh treatment of their oppressors. 'This will always be a blessing to you,' he tells them. 'But,' he warns, 'if the white man tries to use it, it will become, for him, a curse!' I wonder why the 'white man' cannot deal with his own problems at home rather than punishing, again, those who are too weak to defend themselves?

Anyway, I am committed to the translation, doing the best I can and secretly taking the edge off some of the more outlandish comments as they turn into Spanish. The second day is not quite so abrasive and I feel a bit more comfortable. At least it is taking my mind off the problems in the church and, who knows, I might pick up a few helpful tips for dealing with them.

The first talk on the final day is based around John 21. It's the story of Peter's painful reinstatement by Jesus after the Resurrection. Peter has vehemently denied being with Jesus three times, and has heard the dread sound of the cock-crow in judgement. Now, three times Jesus is asking Peter: 'Do you love me?'

I translate the message as best I can, still troubled by the problems which have not gone away. As I hear the words, something begins to change. It is no longer Clancy O'Rourke speaking to this group of leaders. It is no longer Jesus talking to Peter. It is Jesus talking to me. 'Alan, do you love me? Forget all that other stuff for a minute. It can wait. This is the real central issue. Do you love me? Everything else is secondary. This one thing. Do you love me?'

I hear myself saying: 'I have seriously tried my best to serve you Lord, but *love you*? I am not sure what that means. I don't know how to love you.' I struggle on with the translation. Something begins to well up within me. It is as though he's saying: 'Let me show you then.'

Something I do not recognize begins to flood up through my body. 'No! Surely not. I have longed for renewal for a long time, but through this guy? This guy who stands for so much that I despise? Couldn't you use somebody else, Lord? Is this a sick joke?'

But before I know it, I am overwhelmed with a love which is beyond anything I have ever known before. My heart is bursting within me and replying, 'Yes, Lord. I do love you.' Somehow I struggle on with the translation. In fact it seems to be going really well. The words come easily and people are on the edge of their seats. They are experiencing it as well.

The conference finishes. I go back to the same situation. Nothing has changed. Yet everything has changed. Like scales falling from eyes. Like hope renewed. Like love reborn.

> *God forgive me, but I have seen the Holy Spirit at work in places I thought he had no business to be.*
>
> Ian Petit, RC Priest, Carr's Lane Spring Convention, Birmingham, 1972

Sent

I knew God was calling the very best people to serve him in South America. But they weren't responding, so he sent me.

David Pytches, former Anglican Bishop of Chile

I have been trying to persuade some of our church members to go on the 'Cursillo' weekend for nearly a year. I went on it last February. Such a lot of the courses the church puts on seem to need a university degree to understand. So it was refreshing to find something that was led by ordinary people, sharing their own experience of God in an easily accessible way.

I drop off three of our five participants at the conference centre. They are all people who have had a great deal of pain to cope with in their lives, some of it ongoing. They look pretty nervous. I feel pretty nervous myself, but I pretend not to be. I give them a hug and a cheery smile and say I'm sure it will be great. They walk off towards the front door. Some of them have never done this sort of thing before. How will they get on? It's three full days – a long time to hang in there if you don't feel at ease. And it can be pretty intimidating when most of the others seem to be business people, accountants or lawyers and you are on benefits. I say a prayer and hope for the best as I drive off.

Sunday seems a long time coming. At least they haven't done a bunk. Finally, at about 5 p.m. I get a phone call from one of the organizers. 'Yes,' she says, 'they've all completed the course. It was touch and go at first but they finally got into it. And what a blessing they were! They were all so honest and open that everyone else opened up as well. It was brilliant.

Thank you so much for sending them.' Then someone else from the leadership team rings me and says almost exactly the same.

Encouraged by the news, I ring up each of the participants in turn. They are keen to tell me their stories – and keen to share what they've learned with the church. 'Oh,' says one of them, 'we can't stop here. We've been really blessed. I've never felt so loved in all my life. But it's not just for us. We've got to go out and share that love with *everybody*.'

'Look out Holy Cross,' she says. 'Look out East Barnwell. Here we come!'

> *Jesus said to them: 'When the Holy Spirit comes upon you, it will be dynamite! So go out and spread the Good News about me, not just in the Holy Land, but in South America, Uganda, and even East Barnwell!'*
>
> See Acts 1 and 2

Justice

'The Spirit of the Lord is upon me
because He has anointed me to bring good news to the poor.
He has sent me to proclaim liberty for the prisoners
and recovery of sight to those who are blind
to let the victims who have been crushed go free
and to announce that the time of the Lord's welcome has come.'

Jesus said to them: 'Here and now, this prophecy has been fulfilled in your hearing.'

Luke 4.18–21

Watching TV, February 1990

People say the Bible and politics do not mix. Frankly, I don't know which Bible they have been reading.

Desmond Tutu

As we wander through the fruit and veg section my eye catches some delicious-looking Granny Smiths. I pick one up to put in the bag, when my wife's voice, from over my shoulder, says: 'No way! Put them back. We're not buying South African produce until Nelson says it's OK.' I replace them on the shelf and pick up some inferior-looking Cox's instead. It seems such a struggle to forgo these lovely-looking apples in the supermarket. But compared to the sacrifice of so many people's lives . . .

Three years later we sit on the sofa in front of the TV. With hundreds of millions of others, we strain our eyes to catch the first glimpse. The whole place is packed. Vibrant colours fill the streets. The atmosphere is like a coiled spring – a tidal wave of celebration and emotion about to pour forth. Camera crews from every corner of the earth jostle for position.

The crowd suddenly bursts into a deafening roar. Drumming, singing and dancing begin in earnest. It will go on all night and for many to come. The troubles are not yet over. But, at last, tall and upright, relaxed and smiling, unembittered by 27 years of prison, hardship, brutality and loss, embracing freedom fighter and prison warden without distinction, with the eyes of the world upon him, Nelson Mandela walks free.

> *God give us courage to break down hatred.*
> *God give us courage not to be bitter.*
>
> South African Freedom Song

Watching TV, November 1992

> *The women's movement and post-modern culture has done more for me as a woman than the Church ever did.*
>
> Ann Morisy

It has been a gruelling and bruising few weeks. Tensions have been high with talk of the Church being split from top to bottom and of mass desertion. In the heat of it I read a document called *After November* produced prior to the Synod vote by the women deacons of Ely Diocese. I am expecting it to say: 'If they don't vote for women priests we'll go on strike, withdraw our labour, picket the churches and burn our bras.' (Well maybe not that, but I have already imagined the tone.)

As I read, however, I am struck by the astonishing humility of the document and its honest attempt to face the painful possibility of a 'No' vote. Should we accept the pain and continue working? Can we do this without bitterness or a 'martyr complex'? Should we leave ordained ministry and opt for a different career? Can we do this when we feel God's call so strongly and see the ongoing needs of Church and society before us? Should we join another denomination or minister abroad where women priests are already accepted? Should we pursue protest action?

They turn again to the words of the Roman Missal: 'May we come to share in the divinity of Christ, who humbled himself to share in our humanity.' In the midst of their concerns for themselves they think of the future of the Church and its leaders. 'In addition to pledging our support for one another we also wanted to pledge our support for our two bishops who had already shown their loving concern for us in very many ways.'

As I read this soul-searching document I think of the women deacons I know personally. I find myself saying, like Peter, when he discovers that the Holy Spirit has been poured out on pagans as well as Jews, 'When I realized that God was giving them the same gift he gave us when we believed in the Lord Jesus Christ, who was I to stand in God's way?' (Acts 11.17).

We sit on the same sofa and watch the TV. The debating chamber doors are closed. The tellers go to stand by each door: Clergy Ayes, Laity Noes, etc. The vote is called and people begin to file out. The bishops stay in the chamber and shuffle into two groups, trying not to look too divided. There needs to be a two-thirds majority in each house. It does not seem likely. Finally the members file back in. The vote is handed to the Archbishop of Canterbury. He looks grave. As usual, he reminds the Synod, the vote will be received in silence. He begins to read out the results. The Bishops, 39–13, clearly in favour. Clergy, 176–74, seems OK. Laity, 169–82. I make a quick mental calculation. It isn't enough. The vote has been lost. But then I hear the Archbishop's voice again. 'The motion is therefore carried by the necessary two-thirds majority in all three houses.' I have miscalculated. They have voted in favour.

The camera pans across the debating chamber. The silence is surreal – as though the sound has gone on the TV. Some people are looking down at their feet, perhaps in prayer. One man stares blankly ahead, into space. Two women hold hands, weeping. We are weeping now as well. There is still a long way to go before the ordinations. But soon, these women will be able to exercise fully the ministry God called and equipped them for, long ago.

> *When Bishop Festo began ordaining women in Uganda it was terrible. After a while the parishes began to say: 'Thank you Bishop, but we no longer wish for a man as our priest. The women are so much better!'*
>
> A Ugandan Anglican Priest

Judgement

'Shout! Lift up your voice like a trumpet. Do not hold back.
Is this the sort of fast that I want to see?
Bowing down in sackcloth and ashes – is that what you call fasting?
Isn't this the sort of worship I desire
to break the bonds of oppression and the yoke of injustice
to let the oppressed go free and snap every shackle
to share your food with the hungry and give a home to the homeless?'
says the Lord.

From Isaiah 58

La Paz Women's Prison, 1982

Alicia has been in jail now for two years. She was unlucky. The guy trafficking the cocaine (an ex-boyfriend) unfortunately had her name in his diary. So she was arrested and charged with being his accomplice. There is no evidence at all against her. But things are not that easy. She is from a poor family and they can't 'oil enough palms' to get her out.

I go to the Central Court of Justice and walk up the steps. Her case records are up on the third floor. I ask to see the clerk of the court. After a long while he turns up. I can see Alicia's file on the top shelf, covered in dust, exactly where it was when I was here a fortnight ago. I try not to become angry. It only makes things worse. We greet one another, shake hands, pass the time of day. Then down to the business. 'Well of course,' he says, 'it's all very difficult. The court officials have been on strike and nothing much has got done. There is a big backlog and this case is not yet top of the list.'

I remind him that this is a young woman who has been in prison nearly two years. As far as I can see there is no evidence against her. Everyone I have talked to agrees that the case will be dropped. 'Can you not put it on the Judge's desk for him to order a release warrant?' I plead. It is clear to me and to him what the problem is, though it is not mentioned directly. He wants 10,000 pesos to move the file. Then there will be another 5,000 here and 10,000 there, 25,000 for that major step and then perhaps a further two or three payments should sort it.

He then brings up another problem. 'The thing is,' he says, 'she hasn't yet paid her "gastos del estado".' I am not clear what these are but he explains that she has now been in prison nearly two years and that involves quite a cost to the state – a sort of 'hotel bill', if you like. I am now incensed. 'But you and I both know that she is innocent! Are you going to put her in prison and charge her for the privilege as well?' I bellow. 'Certainly it's harsh,' he agrees, 'but what can I do?'

I finally leave, boiling inside and feeling I have got nowhere. I am not looking forward to telling Alicia the news. It looks as though she will have to settle down for another few months in jail, at least.

Cambridge, 1997

Shabra and her two children came to England almost eight years ago from Angola. Her daughter was 11 at the time and her son 14. He is now married to a British woman and they have recently had their first child. Shabra's English is still not great and, when she is upset, as she is now, it isn't easy to understand her.

She hands me the letter from the Home Office. It says that all the appeal processes have now been exhausted and she and her daughter have been given two months to leave the country.

'What will you do?' I ask. 'I do not know,' she says. 'I cannot bear the thought of leaving Sam and his wife here with my grandson. And what will become of Esther? She has grown up here. All her friends are English.' She shakes her head. 'What will become of us? What will become of us? What will become of us?' She is terrified of going back.

We make one last effort – her solicitor, our MP (who has done her best), letters to the Home Office and the Prime Minister (who acknowledge our concerns and tell us they have been passed on to the appropriate department), Immigration, who are 'unable to comment on individual cases'.

'Look,' I say to the official, 'whatever the rights and wrongs of the case, they have been here *eight years*. The children have grown up here. To send them back now is plain cruelty.' But, on 17 March, back they go.

After a month I receive one e-mail. Things are not going well. I have not heard from them since.

Lord God, there are many Alicias. There are many Shabras. Come Lord Jesus. Do not delay. Come quickly. Come and judge the earth.

Going Home

Jesus said to Mary: 'I am going to my Father and your Father, to my God and your God.'

John 20.17

Weep not, I shall not die;
And as I leave the land of the dying,
I trust to see the blessings of the Lord
In the land of the living.

Edward the Confessor

It is early morning in northern Argentina and we are outside enjoying the relative cool before the temperature soars, as usual, to the mid-forties and the wind gets up to cover us in the dry, choking dust of the Chaco. Ernesto has stayed with us overnight in Embarcación. It is too far to get from Salta, the state capital where he has been in hospital, to his home village in just one day. He sits patiently, waiting for a passing truck to give him a lift.

Annie talks with him over breakfast. He has throat cancer which cannot be treated, so he is going back home to die.

'Do you have any children?' asks my wife.

'Yes,' he replies with a warm smile. 'Nine. One living and eight with the Lord.'

Then he tells her how all eight of their children died within a fortnight of each other some years ago in a measles epidemic. The only remaining child was born after it ended.

He is at peace and content. He sits patiently, waiting for a truck to arrive. He is going home. Going home to his village to die. Going home to the land of the living, where he knows he will see them all again.

Lord, if anyone has to die this day, let it be me, for I am ready.

Billy Bray, Cornish tin miner and evangelist, died 1868

Postscript: Recognition

He came into the world, the world he himself had created, but his own people did not recognize him.

John 1.10

We draw up, in our beat-up red Ford pickup, in front of the posh hotel in the middle of Salta feeling a bit nervous. We are meeting the Canadian Ambassador who is coming with us to see the development programme 'Iniciativa Cristiana'. The project, under the auspices of the Anglican Church of Northern Argentina, has been going for some years. We are working in the areas of education, health, economic development and land rights. The Canadian government are particularly keen to help with the land rights issue and have donated several hundred thousand dollars to purchase land on behalf of the indigenous people. Efforts to persuade the provincial government to give land rights to the people who have lived there since time immemorial, but who are now threatened by big companies hacking down the forest to grow soya beans and sunflowers, have so far failed.

When we enquire why the Canadian government are so interested in this project we are told: 'Well, we feel we have failed almost completely with regard to our own indigenous people. Perhaps we can at least help with the situation here.'

The visit by the ambassador to an indigenous community, which has just moved to Carboncito, a 5,000-acre plot of land purchased with Canadian government money, has not been welcomed by the provincial authorities. Salta, the state capital, is a prosperous city in a rich valley producing wine and tobacco. 'Dirty indians' on the frontier with Paraguay are not what they want visiting dignitaries to see. But the ambassador has insisted, so here we are.

He has come with his wife and their 10-year-old son, plus chauffeur and embassy limousine. Kevin, my boss, and I greet them. He suggests we set off, us in the truck and them in the limo. 'Oh no,' says the ambassador, 'That would mean we couldn't talk to you on the way. Why don't I go in the truck with Kevin, and Alan can go with my wife in the car?' We all agree, except the four state security police who have been assigned to protect the ambassador. They are covered in confusion. They've only got one vehicle, so how can they protect two cars? We are not convinced that any protection is required, but we suggest that the limo go first, then the Ford pickup, then the police. They reluctantly agree.

Travelling on dirt roads is not conducive to going by convoy. The thick dust billows into the air, making it impossible for following vehicles to see anything. After an hour the vehicles are several miles apart.

There are a number of police-checks along the road, but they have been advised of the ambassador's visit. The chauffeur has been told to ignore the queue at the checkpoint and drive straight past. However, they have overlooked something important. The province of Salta is 'horseshoe' shaped and the road north actually passes through a different province before returning to Salta. No one has thought to inform the provincial authorities in Jujuy.

We arrive at the Jujuy checkpoint. The chauffeur ignores the queue and drives straight up to the barrier, expecting it to be opened for us as before. The guard holds up his hand for us to stop. Two others come out and point their guns at us. The officer swaggers out of the command post. We have made his day. Trying to jump the queue, eh? This should be fun!

He walks up to the car and barks at the chauffeur: 'Documents!' The chauffeur calmly explains that the documents are in the boot. He gets out and walks round the back to get the diplomatic bag, which holds the official credentials. The officer marches round the back of the car with him. Suddenly, he notices the diplomatic number plate, the Canadian flag, the gold lettering on the leather briefcase which says 'Government of Canada, Ambassador to Argentina.'

He quickly runs back to the car and looks in. It's clearly not the chauffeur or the 10-year-old. In a macho society it doesn't occur to him that it might possibly be a woman. He looks straight at me. 'The Canadian Ambassador?' he asks, looking a bit sheepish. 'Yes!' I say, planning to add: 'This is the Canadian Ambassador's car, but I'm not actually the ambassador. He's in a beat-up, red Ford pickup with a guy called Kevin. They are about ten minutes behind us and a few minutes after them there'll be a police escort.'

Unfortunately, I only get as far as 'Yes' before he jumps back. He and his guards snap to attention and give us their very smartest salute. 'An honour to meet you,' he cries. 'Have a safe journey.' The bar is raised. He waves us on. Meanwhile the chauffeur has returned to the car and we roar off through the open barrier, saluting troops, covered in dust, just visible in the mirror.

In about ten minutes the real Canadian Ambassador will arrive in a beat-up, red Ford pickup truck. They will not recognize him. He is in for a hard time!

*

In a different place, 2,000 years before, a young couple walk in awe into the temple precincts. They have come to make the thanksgiving offering for the birth of their tiny son, who is enfolded in the mother's arms. They push their way through the crowds. There are worshippers, priests, teachers, people selling stuff, tourists. All they see is a young couple, Galileans, from a poor background, carrying their baby, trying to find out where to buy the pigeons they need to buy to make the offering.

Only two old people, Simeon and Anna, look and see the Lord of glory, the Prince of Peace, the Messiah, cradled in his mother's arms. Everyone else sees just an ordinary couple with their baby, or maybe nothing at all. Only an elderly man and a frail widow look, and see the Son of God.

He has not gone away. You will find him in the most unlikely places and with the most unpromising people. But you will have to be attentive and listening. You will have to be watching and praying. You will certainly meet him.

But will you recognize him when he crosses your path?

In the crowded street
On the commuter train
I saw his presence there.

In the news flash
In the bleak rain
Was God beyond compare.

Caught up in commerce
In the superstore
I saw him once again.

In the car crash
With the homeless
Was God who shares our pain.

At my wits' end
In the rush hour
Was God who keeps me sane.

Unexpected, uninvited
Long ignored and long rejected
He will come again.

Adam, 1992

References

Adam, D. (2000) *A Desert in the Ocean*, Triangle.
Adam, D. (1992) 'Fleeting Presence', in *Powerlines*, Triangle.
Barth, K. (1949) *Dogmatics*, SCM.
Boff, L. (1986) *Ecclesiogenesis*, Orbis.
Brueggemann, W. (1984) *The Message of the Psalms*, Augsburg.
Camara, H. (1981) *A Thousand Reasons for Living*, Darton, Longman & Todd.
Cocksworth, C. (1997) *Holy, Holy, Holy*, Darton, Longman & Todd.
Eliot, T. S. (1959) *The Four Quartets*, Faber and Faber.
Frost, R. (1973) 'Fire and Ice', in *Selected Poems*, Penguin.
Hinksman, B. (1999) in *Clinical Counselling in Pastoral Settings*, Routledge.
Iona Community Worship Book (1988), Wild Goose Publications.
Keenan, B. (1992) *An Evil Cradling*, Vintage.
Larkin, P. (1990) 'An Arundel Tomb', in *Collected Poems*, Faber and Faber.
Leunig, M. (1993) *A Common Prayer Collection*, Collins Dove.
Merton, T. (trans) (1970) *The Wisdom of the Desert LXXII*, Shambhala.
Thomas, N. (1980) 'Hard God', in *On the Edge of a Truth*, Barclay.
Ten Boom, C. (1976) *The Hiding Place*, Hodder & Stoughton.

Note: the Bible 'translations' are mostly mine, and are possibly, therefore, dodgy.